The Qaba[...]
cal philoso[...]
magical tradition. Its central symbol is the Tree of Life, a resonant metaphor of the balance and interaction of cosmic emanations, culminating in the *Ain Soph Aur*—the Limitless Light and Ultimate Source.

This book takes you on a journey through the branches of the Tree of Life and examines its images and philosophy in relation to astral magic, creative visualization, magic mirrors, Names of Power, the Tarot, Arthurian legends, and much more ...

- Experience inner worlds and adventures
- Achieve past life memory
- Learn to use the Tarot for self-analysis
- Relate the Tree of Life to your daily life
- Learn the techniques of ritual performance
- Explore magic's principles and philosophy
- Use the exercises for practical applications as well as for overall magical/spiritual development
- Relate myths to your own experience
- Design an Arthurian Tarot
- Get to know yourself at the deepest level, and construct an astral Body of Light and a magical name to match

## About The Author

Alan Richardson was born in Northumberland, England in 1951, and has been writing on the topic of magic for many years. He does not belong to any occult group or society, does not take pupils, and does not give lectures or any kind of initiation. He insists on holding down a full-time job in the real world like any other mortal. That, after all, is part and parcel of the real magical path. He is married with four children and lives very happily in a small village in the southwest of England.

## To Write To The Author

If you wish to contact the author or would like more information about this book, please write to the author in care of Llewellyn Worldwide and we will forward your request. Both the author and publisher appreciate hearing from you and learning of your enjoyment of this book and how it has helped you. Llewellyn Worldwide cannot guarantee that every letter written to the author can be answered, but all will be forwarded. Please write to:

Alan Richardson
c/o Llewellyn Worldwide
P.O. Box 64383-681, St. Paul, MN 55164-0383, U.S.A.
Please enclose a self-addressed, stamped envelope for reply, or $1.00 to cover costs.
If outside the U.S.A., enclose international postal reply coupon.

## Free Catalog From Llewellyn

For more than 90 years Llewellyn has brought its readers knowledge in the fields of metaphysics and human potential. Learn about the newest books in spiritual guidance, natural healing, astrology, occult philosophy and more. Enjoy book reviews, new age articles, a calendar of events, plus current advertised products and services. To get your free copy of the *New Times*, send your name and address to:

*The Llewellyn New Times*
P.O. Box 64383-681, St. Paul, MN 55164-0383, U.S.A.

Llewellyn's New Age Series

# MAGICAL
# GATEWAYS

(A New, Expanded, and Revised Publication
of *An Introduction to the Mystical Qabalah*)

## ALAN RICHARDSON

1992
Llewellyn Publications
St. Paul, Minnesota 55164-0383, U.S.A.

FIRST LLEWELLYN EDITION, 1992
Originally published as *An Introduction to the Mystical Qabalah* (The Aquarian Press, 1974)


Cover art by Lissanne Lake
Interior Egyptian illustrations by Billie John


Library of Congress Cataloging-in-Publication Data
Richardson, Alan, 1951-
        Magical gateways / Alan Richardson.
        p.      cm. — (Llewellyn's new age series)
    "A new, expanded, and revised publication of An introduction to the mystical qabalah." 2nd ed. 1981.
    ISBN 0-87542-681-6
    1. Cabala. 2. Magic. 3. Symbolism. 4. Tree of life—Miscellanea. I. Richardson, Alan, 1951- Introduction to the mystical qabalah. II. Title.
BF1621.R53 1992
135′.4—dc20                                          92-17844
                                                          CIP


Llewellyn Publications
A Division of Llewellyn Worldwide, Ltd.
P.O. Box 64383, St. Paul, MN 55164-0383

# LLEWELLYN'S NEW AGE SERIES

The "New Age"—it's a phrase we use, but what does it mean? Does it mean that we are entering the Aquarian Age? Does it mean that a new Messiah is coming to correct all that is wrong and make Earth into a Garden? Probably not—but the idea of a *major change* is there, combined with awareness that Earth *can* be a Garden; that war, crime, poverty, disease, etc., are not necessary "evils."

Optimists, dreamers, scientists ... nearly all of us believe in a "better tomorrow," and that somehow we can do things now that will make for a better future life for ourselves and for coming generations.

In one sense, we all know there's nothing new under the Heavens, and in another sense that every day makes a new world. The difference is in our consciousness. And this is what the New Age is all about: it's a major change in consciousness found within each of us as we learn to bring forth and manifest powers that humanity has always potentially had.

Evolution moves in "leaps." Individuals struggle to develop talents and powers, and their efforts build a "power bank" in the Collective Unconsciousness, the soul of humanity that suddenly makes these same talents and powers easier access for the majority.

You still have to learn the "rules" for developing and applying these powers, but it is more like a "re-learning" than a *new* learning, because with the New Age it is as if the basis for these had become genetic.

*To William G. Gray,*
*for showing me a straight and narrow path,*
*half a lifetime ago*

# CONTENTS

# Preface

This book offers an introduction to the very essentials of magic. It shows magic to be a spiritual system which every person can use to enhance his or her life. The techniques given are tried and tested methods which will, in time, expand the consciousness of the individual—whether that individual is a Christian, a Pagan, or something else, it makes no difference. At the end of the book the reader will have a broad grasp of those major aspects which comprise the Western Esoteric Tradition, as it exists today. More importantly, each reader will also be left with ideas on how this Tradition may be developed in the decades to come, and of the part he or she might play in this development.

The emphasis at all times is upon the individual, and on the efforts that each person must make. The study and practice of magic as described herein requires no membership of any groups, no knowledge of ancient languages, and no worship of any individual, living or dead. I personally belong to no group, have studied the peculiar philosophy of the Qabalah for twenty years without ever once being able to recognize a single Hebrew letter, and have not found that my magic has suffered in any way.

This book is in fact simplistic, and deliberately so. Whether this is an excuse for superficiality and shallowness, or a sincere attempt to get to the root of things, is something that readers must decide for themselves.

Although the practice of magic can enhance and transform a person's life, it is actually in the last conscious moments before death that it receives its full justification. We might call this the Parable of the Two Brothers (or Sisters!). One brother has no interest in magic or any other spiritual system, and scorns it as mere escapism; the other works at magic with all of his heart. At the moment before death, however, two distinctions occur, the *least* important being that the magician has actually got something to look forward to. (And if that proves to be false, as his scornful brother would insist, then after death it hardly matters anyway.) But the truly important distinction is in what the two have to look back upon. Both will have known love, sex, relationships, jobs, careers, profits and debts, laughter and sorrow and children and travel. The magician will have the full range of experience, the same intense memories as his skeptical brother, but on top of these, in areas denied the latter, the magician will be able to look back also upon a life that extended through more than the usual dimensions. The magician will be able to look back upon inner experiences that were nothing less than extraordinary.

In the practice of magic, the student will learn to link with energies and levels of consciousness that can transform his or her life. These energies will come through in a perfectly natural way. In the magical scheme each individual consciousness is part of one great, corporate whole. We are one another, in fact. Changes within the heart and mind of the magician will eventually affect the heart and mind of the whole race. Each person must learn, therefore, that he or she has a responsibility to work magic as brightly as he or she can. In a very true sense, the world, the future, depends upon it.

To say that magic is escapist is nonsense. Real magic requires too much hard work. We might as well criticize top-class athletes for taking up their sports in order to avoid the so-called "realities" of life. We might as well criticize any human attempts at self-improvement in any sphere. No one works harder at life than the magician.

And the astonishing thing about magic is that it always works—though never *when* the newcomer wants, and rarely *how*. Rituals which I performed with specific intent in the mid-70s, for example, finally worked themselves through in the late 80s. Only then, older and wiser, could I see that the timing of this was actually perfect.

The original draft of this book was written while I was still a teen-ager. I say this not as a boast, but as a desperate attempt to apologize for the crassness of the first edition, which was finally published by Aquarian Press in 1974, with the excruciating title *An Introduction to the Mystical Qabalah*. The second edition, written in Morgantown, West Virginia, and which forms the substance of the present text, was partly done under the prompting of certain "inner contacts" that had been nudging at my psyche during the interim years. This present edition, with a mercifully decent title, seeks to bring the whole scheme up to date.

In my early years of magical practice, as an intensely lonely youth (which youth isn't?), I wanted nothing more than to join a group and be taken under the wing of some all-wise and all-knowing Adept. However, circumstances (fate, location, whatever) all seemed to conspire against the possibility, so that I was always forced to work alone. The techniques and notions given herein, then, are essentially those which inspired my often inglorious but never fruitless early years, and which later on gave me the confidence to enter some strange and luminous realms indeed. I never became a great magician. I cannot claim that even now, thirty years later—although in my naughtier moments I sometimes do—but I have seen and experienced some great and wonderful things because of magic, and had my life transformed. Who could ask for more?

So the techniques *do* work. Your lives *can* be enhanced. The effort alone will bring wisdom.

—Alan Richardson
Wessex, England
Beltaine, 1991

# 1
# Magic and Symbols

When I was a youth I borrowed A.E. Waite's *Book of Ceremonial Magic* from the library and walked home in something of a daze. It might have been a portion of the True Cross I held. All the tales about such books came back to me. I thought about the members of the clan Stewart who would wear magically protective bands of iron around their foreheads before they dared to even open the mysterious tome called the *Red Book of Appin*. When I finally got Waite's book home the glamour of the signs, seals and sigils sent me into a trance. I spent hours copying them on to paper or using them in various circumstances hoping for a wondrous effect. I am still waiting, however.

It took a while for me to realize that they did nothing but exercise my draughtsmanship. But all the same, I was sure that soon I would find some *truly* magical symbols which would provide the results I wanted, such as opening doors at a touch, projecting me off into the astral plane, and making me irresistible to women. None of which ever occurred.

Of course I was bemused and befuddled by too much indiscriminate reading on occultism and my own innocence. My gullibility was matched only by that of the writers whose books I had believed in implicitly, both parties believing that certain secret glyphs possessed untold power.

Much later it became clear that symbols have absolutely no power in themselves. Drawings of magical images or electric circuits have no intrinsic power, but by applying the principles they schematize, remarkable results can be obtained. The pentacles which I had so fruitlessly copied became useful only after I had understood their purpose. They *must* be understood to have any value. A person trying to succeed in magic without understanding the symbolism, will be as big a failure as a driver who cannot understand the road signs.

## What is Magic?

Everything hangs upon what one understands by the term "magic." First of all, it is nothing to do with giving individuals incredible powers, any more than that the sole purpose of life is the accumulation of money. So far no one has surpassed the definition of magic as "the art of causing changes to occur in consciousness," but we usually approach the field in such a state of confusion that even such a simple statement makes no sense at all.

The concept of ritual magic tends to evoke two reactions within people. The first (and the one no doubt felt by the reader) is one of intense glamour and romance, even though the student is not quite sure what the topic involves. The second in sheer disbelief and a vague sense of embarrassment.

What we might do here, however, is to answer our own question by looking at these disbelieving types and seeing how they too are practitioners of magic did they but know it.

The first kind of disbeliever is one who has firm religious beliefs of his own and regards anything else as an aberration. Yet a Catholic, for example, in going to Mass, experiences an act of pure ceremonial magic which might be interpreted by the outsider as having cannibalistic overtones, but yet which invariably has a profound emotional impact within the participant. A change has occurred in his consciousness. He feels a little better for it, and closer to God.

The other kind of disbeliever is one who is a rationalist, non-religious, and who is assured that ritual magic plays no part in *his* life. But unless he is the type of person who has never fallen in love even in the slightest degree, he would be very wrong indeed. The act of falling in love is a ceremony of magic in itself, capable of effecting the most far-reaching changes in consciousness of all. The lover has only to smile or cock an eyebrow and depths within the beloved tremble. The couple share little rites and acts and secret words which are nonsense to the outsider but charged with meaning to the lovers. Simple gestures come to have devastating effect. Whatever the outcome of the affair its very existence does something to broaden the psyche of the besotted. Magic at its highest. Changes occurring in consciousness.

The magic we will be studying in this book must be looked at in exactly these terms. The techniques must be seen as means of self-discovery and self-perfection. The ultimate aim of a magician must inevitably be the same as that of any priest: wholeness, both human and Divine. Whether the disciplines produce side-effects in the psychic fields is very much secondary to whether they help make one into a better and wiser person.

It has to be acknowledged at the outset that most people come to magic with some vaguely defined but very strong urge to gain power. The present writer was no exception. Most of us live rather dull lives and exist as dissatisfied and often rather pathetic people. Magic seems to offer a means of by-passing the usual routes to earthly power, and, with a few symbols and a minimum of effort, hints at infinite possibility.

In reality, however, while the infinite possibility is most definitely there, the idea of minimum effort could not be further from the truth.

A true magician is doing no less than aiming for the Ultimate (however he defines that). Metaphorically speaking, magic is a means of turning inside ourselves, grabbing ourselves, and hauling ourselves up by the scruff of the neck to whatever standards we choose to aspire.

We did it all when we were children, in fact. A child evolves and matures into adulthood by copying the grownups, learning from watching them, and by simulating an adult world by means of play. A child adapts to the world by reproducing it in his own terms in play, gradually enlarging his concepts until he can dispense with play-acting adult situations. In similar ways, a magician evolves toward God-hood using rituals designed to reproduce the Inner Worlds. Child to adult, and adult to God, is the evolutionary route; although we all tend to get a little stuck along the way to both.

## The Meaning of Symbols

Where do symbols fit into all this? Again, look at the world around ...

The gestures of a traffic police officer are based upon a definite system. Each arm movement has a symbolic meaning, which if misunderstood can result in serious trouble. Each letter on this page is a symbol that is used to express ideas and thoughts in visible form. These letters are far more potent than any Egyptian hieroglyphs, simply because you can understand them, and because they have an effect upon your consciousness. The formulae and equations used in science express ideas clearly and simply to the user, but remain incomprehensible to the uninitiated. Symbols are a means of communication, a form of shorthand. Nor is there anything esoteric about their application. Poets use them, the blind and the deaf use them, magicians and children also use symbols to link with actualities around them.

Magic symbols work on common-sense principles. How else? Where a magical concept or technique goes against your common sense then leave it and wait either for further understanding, or different techniques. In ritual magic every gesture *must* have a meaning. They are not used for their aesthetic qualities, but because they are physical representations of inner actualities. When a magician formulates, for example, the Qabalistic Cross, he does so because it is a logical, necessary gesture, and not for dramatic effect.

The experienced magician operates on levels of consciousness which are somewhat different from ordinary experience. The only way he can describe these is by using symbols common to us which are lower analogues of that which he is describing. Accounts of primitive people meeting advanced technology and attempting to describe modern artifacts will supply a parallel here. Symbols are a link between the known and the unknown, the outer and the inner.

## The Lesser and Greater Mysteries

This is not to say that occult teachings cannot be assimilated except through metaphors. In magic there are the Lesser and Greater Mysteries. The former are the basic teachings whose intellectual contents are available to all. The Greater Mysteries can only be understood through experience; they cannot be taught in words. The best that can be done is to provide symbols that the student may use as lenses to bring into focus his own blurred intimations of something greater in this world than himself. That is why it is useless searching books for any True Secret. It does not exist. Books and teachers can only give a few inadequate methods to reach the wisdom that is nowhere else but within the seeker.

In one of his books Aleister Crowley lamented that at his initiation he was given no more than a few astrological symbols and trivial details that he knew already. Yet that is all that any genuine group can possibly give—a basic scheme of symbols which the student must learn to develop himself. This is a hard thing to swallow, as we all tend to build up encyclopedic knowledge of rituals and the qualities of super-consciousness, and are inclined to expect more (and more advanced) information, rather than less. Yet what is the value of hoarding occult details if they do not result in some progression of experience? It is like a young child building up a collection of love poems and anecdotes about the beauty of falling in love. He may reach puberty knowing all the symptoms and effects, but this knowledge crumbles beside the reality. Similarly, a student may, by analysis of the symbolism connected with say, Hermes, gain a good idea of what that god is like, but until he actually makes some sort of Hermes contact he will not really *know*.

In Western Magic, then, we can be given no more and no less than two basic symbols: the equi-armed Celtic Cross, and that of the Tree of Life. The rest is up to us, for there is no dogma, no secret teachings, no mysterious Adepts nor anything which can help us avoid doing a great deal of work to expand these from diagrams in a book out to vast potentials within our personal universes.

Ideally, of course, we should finish the book at this point; but human nature being what it is, there is an obligation to guide the student through the mass—some might say the morass—of symbols and techniques within the magical tradition. It must always be borne in mind, however, that no matter how glamorous some of these may seem, there are only two symbols which are important—the circle-cross and the Tree. Without a solid grasp of these, the rest of them are no more than distractions. These are the electrical circuits which we will attempt to energize.

And we must remember that all the images given are products of our own making. When we talk about gods, goddesses, angels and arch-angels, we refer to personifications of abstract qualities, and we are using these figures to give our minds something to "grip onto." These per-sonified images are used to enable us to make contact with benign inner intelligences, but their shapes are entirely of our making. Using one of the more traditional magical systems, for example, we might refer to the Archangel Gabriel, and the element of Water; but in doing so we must remember this: water is a physical parallel of certain qualities within our psyche; the figure of Gabriel is a symbol of these same qualities at a certain level of operation. As we will show later there are other symbols that can be used if the Judaeo-Christian elements are no longer sympathetic, but in any case they are of *our* creation. The point cannot be repeated too often.

## Concept Association

Students who come to the Qabalah for the first time will very quickly find different books contradicting each other concerning allocations of symbols to particular Spheres. The truth is, each source is right in so much as they get results, and it is by concept association that we actually achieve them.

We have all at one time seen the hero in a film force some villain into submission simply by grabbing his holstered gun, without drawing it. Behind this is the basic psychology of concept association. The villain knows that if the gun is drawn, primed, aimed and fired, a chemical reaction will occur which will have an unpleasant effect. Thus a simple gesture evokes powerful feelings of fear. It also shows that we get out of symbols what we put into them. The unknowing would be unafraid of the gun because he would not associate the gesture with instant death.

A flippant example? Not really. The laws of magic are the laws that govern our evolution. It is the magician's task to see these laws in operation in every aspect of life, no matter how apparently trivial or ludicrous.

When we come to work on the images of the Tree of Life and the circle-cross we will pour so much of ourselves into certain areas that when we choose to release it all we can do this and more, and direct our consciousness along chosen lines and with determined intensity. With experience, for example, intonation of the Godname for the sphere of the Sun, should positively inflame us with the sense of Beauty and Perfect Balance which are the qualities of that sphere as it appears upon the Tree of Life. A real change in consciousness. A real piece of magic.

For those who expected powers, occult domination and the rest, this will come as a real disappointment. Yes, it is to be admitted that magic *can* give these if the student were to set his sights so pathetically low, but would it not be better in the long run to aim for real wisdom, understanding and insight into life and living?

If nothing else, magic can give a certain sparkle back to modern life. It gives us a chance to find the *numinous* within the most mundane of events. In a dying, woeful planet it can give us back a little romance, and a glimpse of worlds within and beyond this one. It is not in any sense escapist. Anyone who has labored day after day at all the numerous facets of magic, both intellectual and practical, and who has paid the tolls that magic will inevitably demand, and who has, on top of all this, got on with his workaday job and tried to make a good life for his family (no easy matter either) will know that the real escape is to keep one's head down and ignore all thoughts of spiritual possibility. The magical path is lonely and hard and has to walk in parallel with the routine one—which is lonely and hard enough in itself.

In different ways we need magic more than we have ever done. The Swiss psychologist

C.G. Jung had a tower of his own design built on the edge of a lake, at Bollingen. There were no modern amenities within this tower, and it was shut off from the modern world. He wanted to keep in touch with his elemental nature and he would go there when he felt the urge to write, commune with himself, or be alone. In old age he would still chop his own firewood, do his own cooking, and have conversations with his pots and pans as he did so. To him it was vital that Western Man re-discover magic. He saw life in terms of myths and rituals and the religious quest. Over and above all the self-styled Adepts and Hierophants, Jung was by far the greatest magician of this century. And he was entirely self-taught, with not the slightest hint of Tibetan Lamas, Space People, or Arabian mystics guiding him from secret sanctuaries c/o Post Office boxes.

And finally, for those people who are attracted by magic but who still have so-called "rational" objections to the talk of gods and goddesses and angels, we can take comfort from Brodie-Innes' statement which I quote here from memory: "Whether gods and demons really exist or not is beside the point; the important thing is that the universe behaves as though they do." With that statement in mind and with the magical scheme regarded as a paradigm, we can go a long way indeed. In whichever direction we choose.

# 2
# The Magical Philosophy

At this point we must look at what is meant by the term "Qabalah." Simply, it is from the Hebrew "QBL," which can be translated in the sense of "from mouth to ear," implying oral tradition. Alternative spellings include "Kabbalah" and "Cabala." The system with which we are dealing, however, is a modern development which revolves around the glyph known as the Tree of Life. The system of emanations depicted by this glyph is by no means the only aspect of the Qabalah, but is the one which offers the most scope for development along our present lines.

The system was evolved into its present form by occultists within the "Order of the Golden Dawn" and similar groups. It is not, as some would hint, antediluvian, nor pre-Christian, nor even pre-medieval. From a purist's viewpoint the Qabalah of twentieth- century occultism bears little resemblance to that described in the Zohar.

Which is only right and proper. Our spelling, our dress, our music, our mores, our style all develop through the centuries and so must our magic. There are many technical terms used within the scheme which are of Hebrew origin, and likewise many images. But bearing in mind all that we have said about using symbols, these can be no more than "empty vessels" waiting for us to fill them with our own essence. We must not think that we are getting subtly involved in any form of Judaism. Hebrew is used here as Latin is used by the medical fraternity. And as we shall see later, there is no reason why we should not eventually and completely Anglicize or Celticize or re-interpret the Qabalah entirely in the idiom of one's own country. Indeed it may well be waiting for each man to do that.

However, before this ambitious step should be taken, we should look at what other people have done with the glyph so far, so that we may determine how best we may improve upon it—when we are experienced.

In this book, however, it will only be possible to give the basics of the philosophy behind the Tree. Anything more would bog the reader down too soon. Serious students will necessarily hunt out the more advanced works and progress of their own accord.

So what is the Tree of Life?

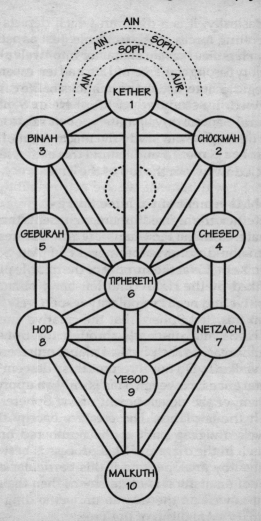

*Figure 1. The Tree of Life*

Basically, it is a diagram which depicts the operating forces of the universe. Just as astrology classifies human character into twelve distinct types, so the Tree of Life has ten essential categories into which the qualities of life can be divided. By studying each Sphere or Sephira (plural Sephiroth) separately, or in relation to the others, we can study the mechanism of life on every plane. To understand this better, let us work down from the top of the Tree.

### The Movement of Creative Energy

Kether, the highest Sphere, represents the Ultimate, God, the First Cause, which manifested from the absolute Nothingness of Ain Soph Aur. Kether is at the summit of the middle pillar flanked by the right- and left-hand pillars of positive and negative polarity respectively. It is from this first Sphere that the creative energy proceeds and descends through the Spheres until it reaches the physical plane, represented by Malkuth. Do not interpret this "descent" in literal terms, however. This is only an approximation of the development of the Spheres on the various planes. The creative energy then travels a zigzag path in the numbered order shown in the diagram. This process is best described by analogy, and if this particular concept of emanation is understood, then the student is well on the way to understanding the primary symbolism of the Tree.

Imagine, therefore, a trail of inflammable chemical substances of graded densities, each in contact with the next in line. The finest substance at one end represents Kether, while the densest at the other is Malkuth. The remaining Spheres are represented by the intermediate substances.

Picture, then, a flame applied to the Kether-ic chemicals. As it travels down the line, the flame changes in quality and character, according to the nature of the different chemical reactions.

If one transmutes this analogy to its spiritual equivalent, one should have a rough idea—a very rough idea—of the basic emanationist theory (realizing, of course, that the passage of the "flame" is a continuous process).

Just as each chemical in our analogy produced a different quality flame, so does each Sphere generate a different quality of spiritual force affecting life of every kind and degree.

## Balancing Forces

So each Sphere is endowed with certain characteristics which affect us here on Malkuth, the physical plane. To illustrate this, let us look at Chesed and Geburah.

Chesed represents constructive energy, genial forces as described by the word "Mercy" in its widest sense. Geburah, its diagrammatic opposite, is symbolic of destructive energy, the cleansing, scourging forces necessary to counteract Chesed. Chesed builds up forms, whether in the field of houses or character; Geburah smashes these down when they have outlived their usefulness. And then Chesed steps in again to build bigger and better houses or characters on the old ruins. Look at the Great Fire of London for a physical example. For spiritual examples, look at how man learns, from seemingly catastrophic events shattering his security, to build up a better, more mature character.

In English terms, Chesed and Geburah are known in their abstracts Mercy and Justice. They are balanced by the Beauty and Perfect Balance of Tiphereth, which means Love.

The same idea applies to the other twins Binah-Chockmah, and Netzach-Hod.

The opposite forces of the outer Spheres find their balance in the Spheres of the middle pillar, and in this action there is an important lesson to be learned. The lesson is that man must build a balanced personality before he can safely tackle the most practical aspects of the Mysteries. He must learn to balance his own internal forces by counteracting any undesirable traits with their opposing influences. The archetypal hippies, for example, could do with a good dose of Hodic reason and logic to balance them.

Of course this is a simplified explanation. Some might say over-simplified. But it must be remembered that the point of this book is not to give the reader a thorough grounding in the philosophy behind the Tree. Instead, it is an attempt to show how magical techniques and systems are *derived* from the Tree. The following descriptions of the Spheres are meant as guidelines only.

So now we will study the Tree of Life, starting at the Source.

### Ain Soph Aur

This is perhaps the hardest concept to grasp, because there are no concrete ways to describe it. It is the most abstract concept of all, but also the most important, for it is out of Ain Soph Aur that *all* proceeds.

To translate, it means—Ain: *Nothingness*. Ain Soph: *Limitlessness*. Ain Soph Aur: *Limitless Light*.

In character, it is Absolute Nothingness, preceding even Kether. We cannot posit it by juggling words around. We can only attempt to gain some sort of rudimentary understanding, and hope to grow in it.

In Eastern terms, it is Nirvana. But that does not mean that we are talking about a mystical experience; it is only such when man achieves it. Ain Soph Aur is the source from which Everything manifests. Those familiar with the Theosophical writings may know the concept of the "Days and Nights of Brahma." This idea states that at vast periodic intervals, the whole of the manifest universe returns to the source of Nothingness. This is the Unmanifest, the Veils of Negative Existence, or Ain Soph Aur.

The light analogy is used because light is the most abstract, unsubstantial symbol capable of equating.

Try and picture this absolute nothingness becoming denser at a focal point, until Kether, the First Sephira, or Sphere manifests. Kether becomes the Limitless Light in Extension.

Confusing? Vague? Undoubtedly. But don't be deterred. No one can understand this concept fully without experiencing it, and to do this means to transcend God-hood even.

But where does this all lead us? What is the practical importance of this concept?

The earlier definition of magic stated that the magician uses ritual to create a spiritual cosmos within him. Thus when we study and apply the Absolute Nothingness of Ain Soph Aur within ourselves as far as is possible, anything then proceeding from consciousness will be unhampered by other concepts, because there *is* no other concept beyond this one. Thus Nothingness will form the absolute bedrock of your knowledge and understanding. It will become the one complete certainty upon which to rely. Anything directed from your mind during the ritual will be pure and unsullied by overlapping influences. Or such is the basic ideal, anyway.

When we come to symbols and images relating to this, we will find Ain Soph Aur conspicuously absent from the appendix at the back of this book. Any image must necessarily be too concrete for the concept of Negative Existence, of Nothingness. All we can use are images of the most nebulous kind, such as a simple circle, or the glyph for infinity, with the node representing Kether. However, most of the symbol-application we will be studying concerns the Spheres, so we will now turn to Kether.

## Kether

The word *Kether* means the Crown. It is indeed the crown of the Tree. The word suggests the kingly qualities of power, wisdom, justice and every other quality the archetypal king should possess.

Kether equates with omnipotence, omniscience, and the First Cause. It is called variously the Ancient of Days, the Most High, and Macroprosopus and others.

Situated at the top of the Middle Pillar of Equilibrium, Kether represents the absolute perfection of God. As it is the first Sphere from which all the others manifest, it contains the perfected essence of all of them.

Its spiritual experience is Union with God, after which is only Nirvana. But we must not think that Kether is the "best" of the Spheres. Qabalistic teaching asserts that each is as spiritually necessary, and therefore as holy, as the rest, that Malkuth is as holy as Kether.

There is a wide variety of symbols for Kether, and these will be dealt with separately. Here, we are just concerned with their natures and qualities. This said, we move to

## Chockmah and Binah

*Chockmah* means "Wisdom." It is at the top of the positive, or masculine pillar, with all that these words imply in their absolute or archetypal senses. It is power of Kether in dynamic action, stimulating and energizing Binah.

*Binah* means "Understanding," and is situated opposite Chockmah at the top of the negative, or feminine pillar. It is receptive to the flowing power of Chockmah, and is known as the "Great Sea," or "Great Mother." Chockmah being the Supernal Father, the analogy with human sexuality is obvious. Remember though, that the physical worlds are dim reflections of the spiritual, not vice versa.

Chockmah and Binah, therefore, are force and form respectively.

In human terms, Binah equates with everything related to stability of form serving to provide life. That is, Binah is the archetypal Womb, the archetypal Temple. Chockmah is the force which energizes these forms.

Remember though, that as yet they are only the *ideas* of force and form, which materialize as actualities on lower levels.

## Chesed and Geburah

*Chesed* (also known as Gedulah) means Mercy, or Compassion. As we noted earlier, it is concerned with up-building forces.

*Geburah*, which relates to Strength, Severity and Justice, breaks up, destroys and tempers *with* Justice the vices of Chesed-ic over-indulgence. It is a corrective force in the highest sense.

In human terms, the misuse of the Chesed-ic forces can lead to self-indulgence, hypocrisy, and bigotry. Similarly, Geburah misused can result in cruelty and senseless vandalism and destruction. This is where the idea of balance is necessary, else chaos will result.

The planets Mars and Jupiter are assigned to Geburah and Chesed respectively. The association of Mars with the forces of war is obvious. The word "martial" typifies the nature of Geburah. It expresses the violent energy, determination and rigid discipline of this sphere. Jupiter, meanwhile, relates to fatherliness, protectiveness, and joviality as opposed to the sternness of Mars.

Geburah teaches us that it is sometimes necessary to suffer certain hardships which change our lives, our characters. Chesed helps us regain our stability after these events, and build again from the ashes of the old.

## Tiphereth

This Sphere balances the forces of Chesed and Geburah. It is the central sphere on the Tree, and it relates to Beauty, Harmony, and Perfect Balance. It possesses in balanced form the benevolence of Chesed and the fierceness of Geburah.

It relates to the higher mental consciousness, as opposed to ordinary psychism, and its spiritual experience gives a vision of the harmony of things, and the mystical symbolism of sacrifice and crucifixion.

Its planet is the Sun, which can nurture or destroy with its heat. Sun-types can be proud, conceited and egotistical, but they can also be devoted people imbued with a great determination.

Tiphereth relates to Christ, and other Sun-gods, and is given titles such as The Lesser Countenance, The Son, and others.

## Netzach and Hod

*Netzach* means "Victory," while *Hod* means "Glory."

If Hod is the Sphere of the Intellect, then Netzach is the Sphere of Emotion. As such, Hod governs ceremonial and ritual magic, while Netzach is concerned with elemental and nature contacts.

Netzach relates to the senses and passions, the sheer thrill of living and enjoyment of instinctual pleasures. Its planet is Venus, goddess of love and all things natural. Netzach is everything in the personality which is spontaneous and instinctive. Its spiritual experience is vision of Beauty Triumphant.

At its higher levels, Netzach is characterized by unselfishness of love, but again, there are the lower levels of sheer animal sensuality and "living for kicks."

Hod is the Reasoning Mind, the mind of the cold, hard intellectual incapable of emotions—unless it is balanced by Netzach, that is. It is a Sphere of logic and insight, truthfulness and inspiration, as well as the falsehood and trickery arising out of high degrees of cunning.

Its planet is Mercury, which rules messages, eloquences of speech and everything that the term "mercurial" suggests. The Greek equivalent Hermes is responsible for the magical arts being referred to as "hermetic," for remember this is the Sphere of ritual magic.

## Yesod

*Yesod* means "Foundation." It relates to the subconscious mind which is the basis, or foundation, of our personality, and also to the etheric substance which is the foundation of life. Yesod balances Hod and Netzach, just as Tiphereth balances Chesed and Geburah.

The governing planet is the Moon, which reflects light on to us from the Sun (which Sun?).

The tides of the ocean and the human soul are guided by the Moon. It is said to influence the growth of planets, and is linked with the periods of women.

It is the Astral Light—impressionable and malleable—which holds the images and fantasies created by our minds, and this is the nature of Yesod, which is also the group-soul or *anima mundi*. The virtue of Yesod is independence, the independence of one who has outgrown the need for others to support him, physically, emotionally, mentally and spiritually. This is the independence needed on the occult path. It is the realization that you and *only you* can get inside yourself and do your evolving; it is the realization that evolution will mean some hard work. Not surprisingly, the main danger at Yesod is that of idleness, which makes the neophyte delay in taking the path, makes him put it off until he loses momentum, and grinds to a halt.

## Malkuth

Malkuth, the Kingdom, is the physical world. It is the final Sphere, absorbing the qualities of the others, and giving physical form to the less material forces.

Malkuth is not related to a particular element, but contains them all, because the four elements together are essential to Malkuth's existence. Thus operations involving the Earth-force should be directed at Netzach, where Auriel and Venus are symbols of growth and fertility. More of this later though.

One of the inner aspects of Malkuth is connected with the etheric plane and the act of dying, for one of the titles of Malkuth is The Gate of Death.

The basis of ritual magic is in Malkuth, for the physical symbolism in connection with the mental and emotional forces of Netzach, Hod and Yesod attempts to take the magician even higher up the tree.

### The Hidden Sephira—Daath

And now we are going to shock you by mentioning Daath, the "hidden Sephira." This is the dotted line in between Kether and Tiphereth.

Modern Qabalists are of the opinion that this is another Sphere and there is a great deal of dispute about its purpose and symbolism. We must mention it here because it has a momentary relevance to the Middle Pillar exercise dealt with later.

Essentially, Daath is the bridge over the Abyss which separates Divinity from that which is not quite divine. The Abyss prevents anything less than perfect from reaching the upper triad. It *can* be crossed by means of Daath, which means Knowledge—the knowledge of experience. This is all we really need to know for our practical purposes.

## Relating Your Experience to the Tree

So now we have worked briefly through the Tree of Life. Remember that *every* aspect of experience can be categorized into one or more of the Spheres, and we must try to do this with the things in our world. We may see a stern father, for example, spanking a particularly unruly child. This would be seen as Geburah in action. Later we may see the same man filled with compassion and forgiveness and decide that this is Chesed. And finally, we may see father and son reconciled and happy, and be sure that this is Tiphereth, the Sphere of Harmony, making its presence felt within the pair of them. A doctor, receiving a call on the telephone before driving over to use his skills to heal someone's wounds, is an example of Hod in action, the planet Mercury relating to communication, travel, intellect, and healing of hurts and wounds. A young boy composing a love letter and plotting ways in which he can just happen to bump into his fancy and all the while wrestling with his nascent lusts is an example of Hod, Netzach and Yesod at work. Bearing in mind Binah's title of "Sorrow" and the name, which means "Understanding," we can appreciate that the highest qualities of the latter can arise if we can cope with our suffering and sorrows. While in terms of the dynamic energies of Chockmah, we might ponder Blake's saying: "The roads of excess lead to Wisdom."

A study of astrology here is a great advantage, the character of each planet relating to its Sphere. In practical magic we can use this to our benefit. For example, a ritual dealing with the forces of Geburah would take place on Tuesday (ruled by Mars) at the specific *hour* ruled by Mars. Now whether there really are cosmic forces around at those times which will aid our rituals is not important. By choosing to perform the ritual according to this scheme you are adopting a particular frame of mind from which it will be easier to, so to speak, "take off."

Of course, we can begin to see the Tree of Life now on several levels: macrocosmically it represents the structure of the universe and the forces which shape our lives; microcosmically it represents the inner structure of Man and the qualities of the Self which attempts to assert itself against the Universe. This is just a restatement of "As above, so below." Man is a miniature of the universe.

## The Importance of Numbers and Colors

Although there is an entire branch of number study known as the *gematria*, it is something that I feel is of only limited importance to the modern magician. On a more simplistic level we can note that each Sphere is numbered in order of descent, so that Chesed is four, and Netzach seven. Thus a square would symbolize Chesed, and a beautiful seven-pointed star Net-

zach and Venus. Anyone working in the latter
Sphere might, perhaps, have seven candles arranged into the star-shape for the same reasons
we gave above relating to rituals dealing with
martial forces. Further, at the end of a ritual, a
magician usually gives ten knocks on the floor.
As he does so he visualizes the Spheres in order,
willing himself to descend in consciousness
back to the levels of Malkuth, the tenth Sphere.

Colors also have a place of some importance.
Each Sphere has its own particular color "frequency," as we might term it. In the advanced
studies on the topic will be found complex and
comprehensive charts, but here we need do no
more than give a basic outline. We might add at
this point also that this is by no means a science.
Many popular occultists tend to imply that a
certain color means a certain thing, but too
much emphasis on this leads us very close to
trivializing the whole topic. So colors for the
Spheres as given here should be regarded in the
same light as any other symbol.

Malkuth, traditionally, is given the four colors of citrine, olive, russet and black, which hint
at the different colors of the Elements as they
appear in nature.

Yesod is given the colors of silver-violet, or
violet-blue, to capture the peculiar qualities of
moonshadows.

Hod is given the color of orange to express
the quality of intellect, while Netzach balances

it with green, for this Sphere has connections with the peculiar emotions that beautiful countryside can inspire in us.

Tiphereth is traditionally given the color of rose-pink, flecked with gold, but this is so much the sphere of the Sun that any brilliant visualization of this orb will suffice.

Geburah, the martial sphere, is obviously equated with red, while Chesed has the more tranquil color of a rich blue.

Binah, the sphere of Sorrow, is colored black, while Chockmah nearest to God is given as iridescence.

Kether itself is beyond mere color, and is ascribed the quality of utter brilliance.

Thus returning to what we said about the Geburah ritual, we can expand it more and have it take place on a Tuesday, at the hour of Mars, with red as the dominant color within the color, and the pentagon as the dominant symbol.

## The Names of Power

These, quite understandably, fascinate most people. We are still hooked into the concept that there might, after all, be some magic word which can do everything for us. The Names, like our own names, are no more than keys. If we hear someone calling us, then depending upon who does so, and how they do so, we react inside in different ways. Any teacher knows that the first thing he must do with any class is learn all the names. That is the first step toward gaining any real discipline and (eventually) affectionate response from them. There is a theory that the Names are designed to stimulate the psychic centers (chakras), which seem to have physical correspondences with the endocrine glands, but we will mention this more in a later chapter. More likely their value is that they are, at present, "none sense" words which we will deliberately fill with the highest concepts we can imagine. Like very private pet names, in fact. When intoned during the working the aim is to tune into the particular energies being invoked and change our consciousness, for the duration of the rite, into that frequency.

Speech as a whole should be adapted to the nature of the Sphere concerned. Normal conversational tones for Malkuth, stern tones for Geburah, and an awestruck whisper for Kether.

So we can see from this that everything can be interrelated and interconnected. Everything must point toward the same idea so that the mind can concentrate its force into definite channels of pin-point intensity. The degree of concentration needed is very great, and naturally there is an early tendency to rush things. But they should be done carefully and slowly however, so that the full force of visualization can be exerted. For it is the visualized images behind the ritual gestures which are important.

They give power to the gestures and achieve reality within the Astral Light, which is the same as the unconscious mind.

## Expanding Ourselves

But why? Someone must still be asking. *Why* raise our consciousness to the levels of Chesed? What will happen?

Harking back to what we said about magic being primarily a means of making us into better, wiser people, then surely any extension of consciousness, any development in experience will serve to broaden our minds, to use a very trite phrase. One can take a lesson here from *A Christmas Carol* by Charles Dickens. Scrooge existed for much of his adult life in a state of meanness, bitterness, and downright cruelty. Suddenly, after a most extraordinary extension of consciousness, he found himself able to function in other, beneficent areas. He found himself pushed into the realm of Jupiter, or Chesed, with its largess, its humanity, and its sense of humor. No one can deny that a change in his consciousness did not make him into a better man. The only difference is that in our case, magic is a voluntary process.

# 3
# The Cross and the Elements

The other main glyph used within the Western Magical Tradition is that of the circle-cross, the Celtic cross, the equi-armed cross of the Elements, to give it various names. It is no more than a circle equally divided by a cross inside it, yet it is as all-encompassing as the Tree of Life itself.

In the Tree, Malkuth is known as the Sphere of the Elements. This, in fact, is our circle-cross. All of the magical operations made possible by the Tree's unique plan necessarily take place within Malkuth. The circle-cross therefore, is our launching-point for ascending the Tree. (The rest of the Spheres fit into this fourfold system rather neatly, but we have saved this for the appendix to avoid clouding the issue here.)

## The Circle Cross

In ancient times in Western Europe, where the seasons are clearly defined, a four-point analysis of heavenly patterns was inevitable. The day was clearly seen to consist of dawn, noon, dusk, and night; the year had sharp seasons of spring, summer, autumn and winter; while the constituent qualities of the world were known to consist of Air, Fire, Water and Earth.

The body, for instance, was Earth; the blood was Water; the breath Air; and the bodily heat was Fire.

Nowadays we might refer to these same Elements as solids, liquids, gases, and radiations, but in so doing we have in no wise superseded the old designation.

It was (and is) only logical to see that these Elements had parallels on different levels which could be extended indefinitely. In Jung's speculations the four modes could be determined as being Sensations (Earth), Feeling (Water), Thought (Air), and Intuition (Fire). While astrologically the twelve signs are grouped into four triplicities which relate to the Elements, thus:

**Fire:** Aries, Leo, Sagittarius
**Air:** Gemini, Libra, Aquarius
**Water:** Scorpio, Pisces, Cancer
**Earth:** Taurus, Capricorn, Virgo

We can see within this particular ordering of the Elements a distinct staging process of increasing density from Fire downward. This relates to the so-called "Four Worlds" of the Qabalists, which we can categorize as follows:

| Fire | Atziluth | Emanation |
| Air | Briah | Creation |
| Water | Yetzirah | Formation |
| Earth | Assiah | Action |

We can see this at work in the urge to paint a picture, perhaps. A spark (Emanation) is struck within the artist's psyche which is nearly imperceptible, Unmanifest Thought, almost. Yet it gradually expands into vague but powerful impulses to paint (Creation) which eventually begin to shape into specific designs (Formation) and are brought to fruition after much physical effort (Action).

So this shows that the Elements can also be used to refer to the most subtle and intangible aspects of our thoughts. They refer then, to the four bases of our physical and spiritual worlds. Were we to make a brief list of correspondences so far it would look like this:

Fire/Radiations/Summer/Leo/Wand/Emanation
Air/Gases/Spring/Aquarius/Sword/Creation
Water/Liquids/Autumn/Scorpio/Cup/Formation
Earth/Solids/Winter/Taurus/Shield/Action

The list can obviously be extended infinitely, and in a later chapter we will add a few more attributions, but there is sufficient there to show that the actual physical elements are worthless in themselves. The important thing is that when you stand at one of the quarters of the magic circle there will be a vast range of concepts in your mind relating to that quarter, giving it an impact within you.

The design of the circle-cross is a mandala, a symbol of the psyche in perfect equilibrium. It is what we aspire toward when we come to practice magic. A person who is essentially "airy" for example, should make more efforts to bring out of himself more of the other Elements. His aim, after all, is to become Whole. The design is also the basis of most group ritual—that is, workings along inner lines with other sympathetic people. But we will leave a discussion of that for another chapter.

## Four God-Forms

Traditional magic uses the images of four archangelic figures placed at the Quarters of the circle-cross: they are Raphael, Michael, Gabriel, and Auriel. These are the main god-forms for much magical working.

There are two main ideas as to what these images actually do.

First, there is the idea that by energizing these figures (which, remember, are personifications of qualities within our own psyches) with the highest aspects of our selves, we are, in effect, sending out a signal into the inner worlds. At a certain point this will be answered by evolved and specialized inner entities who can judge by the quality of this signal that they might want to associate with and help us. The images are thus seen as points of contact between this and the otherworld, and are used by the entities as vehicles, for the duration of the working. In a *very* crude sense it is like advertising one's qualities in a newspaper in the hope of attracting a suitable partner who might share your ideals, although it would not be wise to push that analogy too far.

The second theory holds that these images push through instead into the Collective Unconscious, and that what comes through are selected aspects of the racial group-mind. It is as though we could tap those parts of the genetic structure (if that is the right term) which contain all of man's unconscious inherited learning.

There are many other theories but these are the two main ones. But as to which theory is a more likely explanation as to what the Gods really are, I frankly don't worry.

The traditional archangels of the Quarters, then, are:

| | | |
|---|---|---|
| Raphael | East | Sword |
| Michael | South | Wand |
| Gabriel | West | Cup |
| Auriel | North | Shield |

They are invariably described as follows:

*Raphael*. Predominantly a yellow-orange figure, young with sharp intelligent eyes, he wears a short Grecian-style tunic for ease of movement (in another guise he is Mercury, god of travel). In his hand is a large sword and emblazoned on his cloak is a caduceus, which you can glimpse as the wind flutters the cloak, for Raphael, god of Air, is a wind-blown figure.

*Michael*. A figure clad in the colors of Fire, golden-haired, strong, and radiant. He wears a breastplate emblazoned with a lion's head and carries a spear. He is sensed as being a strong, energetic figure, and one who can be as uncompromising as he is helpful.

*Gabriel*. Clad in long robes of shades of blue and violet. His face is pale with deep-set features. He holds aloft a silver goblet and is surrounded by a sense of Water. His is the type of character one would term "deep."

*Auriel*. The colors of nature are his, for his Element is the Earth, so his long robes are olive-green, brown, citrine and russet, trailing the ground around him. In his hand is a shield which is understood to represent a portion of the Earth's curvature, while emanating from him is a sense of growth and fertility.

Now although we have used the masculine gender for all of these god-forms it is clear that gods themselves must react with goddesses. So Gabriel and Auriel should ideally be given a sense of feminine qualities. A young and mature woman respectively, perhaps. Or in this feminist age there is no reason why these qualities cannot be ascribed to the two positive Elements of Air and Fire. It is up to the user to determine what *feels* right, regardless of what his head tells him. We shall be suggesting an alternative scheme to this in a later chapter anyway.

## The Magical Weapons

We have mentioned the four Weapons in passing several times. These are the means—the tools—through which the god-forms find active expression.

*The Sword.* Of all the four instruments this is the only one which does not have an obvious natural equivalent, unless it be in the crude form of a piece of jagged flint, or similar. The sword was the weapon which required the furthest leaps of proto-science to achieve. It required a degree of intellect and application that was little short of wondrous. We shall come back to this weapon's significance in a later chapter, but meanwhile we might mention W.G. Gray's speculation that the sword was originally an arrow—an obvious Air attribution. The quality of the sword is that it can cut through obstacles just as surely as reason and logic can cut through many problems.

*The Wand*. Both a staff which can aid the traveler and an offensive or defensive weapon. Early, natural versions of the wand, or spear, were just fire-hardened sticks. They were used also in the control of fire, either as pokers, or as torches in themselves.

We can see here that arrow and spear are but different-sized versions of the same thing. Indeed, were we to view the magical universe in purely dualist terms then it would be one of Black and White, or Fire and Water. In the present scheme, however, Fire and Air are seen to be aspects of the same, positive, dynamic energy. Which brings us to their counterparts:

*The Cup*. Apart from the associations with the Holy Grail which we will go into later, the cup was originally the cauldron, the communal bowl from which the tribe drew its nourishment and also learned something about being social creatures. The very life of the tribe came forth out of the pot, as the fruit of love came from the womb.

*The Pentacle*. The shield, or pentacle (or pantacle) was, according to Gray, a piece of material used for scraping the surface of the earth as an early spade, for the planting of seed. This was the tribe's insurance and protection against famine. Again later on, we shall see something of the shield's peculiar link with the concept of sacred stones. Both represent endurance, protections and the Earth itself.

Again we can see that a cup is but a version of the shield folded more into itself—or conversely so. They are complementary energies.

## Circle-Cross Correspondences

So, anticipating some of the later chapters a little, we might now expand the list of fourfold attributions given earlier and see what we have:

| Sword | Wand | Cup | Shield |
|---|---|---|---|
| East | South | West | North |
| Dawn | Noon | Dusk | Night |
| Spring | Summer | Autumn | Winter |
| Merlin | Arthur | Nimue | Morgana |
| Raphael | Michael | Gabriel | Auriel |
| Life | Light | Love | Learning |
| Thought | Intuition | Feeling | Sensation |
| Hearing | Sight | Taste/Smell | Touch |
| Air | Fire | Water | Earth |
| Aquarius | Leo | Scorpio | Taurus |
| Man | Lion | Eagle | Bull |

And so on ad infinitum.

As can be seen, the more the student works at it, the greater the number and pressure of the concepts that build up behind a single key image such as the Magical Weapon is intended to be. When a magician takes up his wand (or rod or spear) and holds it aloft in a particular way, it is a signal to his unconscious to unleash the vast hoard of wand-qualities within the magician's psyche.

Ideally, of course, the student will go on to make actual physical versions of these, but without this preliminary work on the concepts that will "charge" the Weapons, they will be no more than useless.

At this moment however, having given basic overviews of the Tree of Life and the Celtic Cross, let us look in some detail at an actual and traditional piece of magical working.

# 4
# The Middle Pillar

The basis of this chapter is the exercise of the Middle Pillar. This technique, when analyzed, shows the basis of most Qabalistic magic.

Look at Figure 2. This shows the Microcosmic Tree of Life. It is a symbolic representation of the Tree within the human body.

What we are specifically concerned with is the Middle Pillar. The Spheres of this pillar coincide with the top of the head (Kether); the throat (Daath); the solar plexus (Tiphereth); the genitals (Yesod); and the feet (Malkuth).

Those of you familiar with yogic systems will be aware that these locations bear close relationship to the chakras. More precisely, the chakras relate as follows:

| | |
|---|---|
| Muladhara Chakra | Malkuth |
| Swadisthana Chakra | Yesod |
| Manipura Chakra | Tiphereth |
| Anahata Chakra | Tiphereth |

| | |
|---|---|
| **Visuddhi Chakra** | Daath |
| **Ajna Chakra** | Daath |
| **Sahasrara Chakra** | Kether |

The Muladhara Chakra is "removed" from the base of the spine to beneath the feet, where it is regarded as a storage center.

The aim of the exercise is to circulate force within the aura, to vitalize it and charge it. Once this is done, the energy can be turned to achieve specific ends which we will deal with in turn.

Look at the charts. What relates to *Kether* which we can use? Colors? God-names? Qualities? Selecting these we get:

| | |
|---|---|
| *Color* | Brilliant radiance |
| *God-name* | Eheieh |
| | (pronounced *Ehy-hey-eh*) |
| *Characteristics* | Omnipotence, Omniscience; the Creative Power; Perfection |

So, visualize this brilliantly radiant Sphere above your head. Pronounce the God-name rhythmically, and as vibratorily as possible. Imagine the Sphere pulsating with the power of the Name; imagine the inside of that Sphere as the universe itself, pounding and throbbing with the Name; and as you say it, bear in mind the qualities of Kether. Remember this is not a glass sphere, it is alive, swirling with energy.

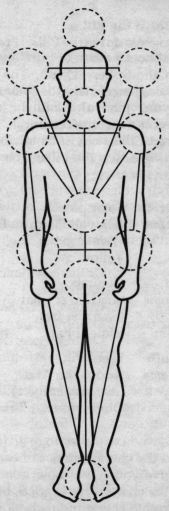

*Figure 2. The Microcosmic Man*

## Moving Down the Pillar

Then progress down the Pillar. From the base of Kether shoots a beam of pure energy which flares into the Sphere Daath. The process is again the same, except that the color is gray, and the God-name Jehovah Elohim compounded from the god-names of Geburah and Binah (pronounced *Yeh-ho-voh El-Lo-heem*).

Continuing down the Pillar, the correspondences are as follows:

> **Tiphereth**   Solar plexus
> *God-name*      Jehovah Eloah va Daath
>                 (*Yeh-hove-vah El-oh vay Daas*)
> *Color*         Yellow
>
> **Yesod**       Genitals
> *God-name*      Shaddai el Chai
>                 (*Shardi el kee*)
> *Color*         Violet-blue
>
> **Malkuth**     Feet
> *God-name*      Adonai ha Aretz
>                 (*Ardonay ha aretz*)
> *Color*         Olive, russet, black

Obviously you will need to re-acquaint yourselves with the characteristics of each Sephira, and also give yourselves new information by searching the charts. This is good, because you will be forced to check and recheck your information until you become thoroughly familiar with it.

To apply the exercise so far, you should be in a room by yourself, lying or sitting relaxed. Hands should be clasped and feet together to complete the "circuit."

## Circulating Force Within the Aura

Now that the chakras are energized, we turn to the task of circulating force within the aura. This is done by combining breathing techniques with visualization—the system in yoga known as pranayama.

Visualize the egg-shaped aura around your body. Then as you exhale steadily, imagine a brilliant force traveling down the *left* side of the aura, from top to bottom. Hold it there. Now, picture this force flowing up the *right* side from bottom to top, as you inhale. Then repeat this several times. The whole picture should be of a band of force in synchronized circulation with your breathing, flowing down one side into the other, and up again.

Then do the same again, except this time the force flows down the whole front of the aura, and up the whole back. Exhalation takes the energy from the head down over the body to the toes, inhalation sucks the energy back up to the head.

The exercise is completed by the "fountain" technique. Having completed the preceding steps, exhale strongly and steadily, visualizing a column of light shooting up through the body from the feet, and out through the top of the head. As it comes out it sprays like a fountain, or like the Sahasrara Chakra as seen by clairvoyants. On inhalation the spray curves down the limits of the aura to the feet again. And so on.

The energy travels up the spine, taking the route of the Kundalini, which may offer a clue to some of you wanting to study it further.

We have now energized our psycho-spiritual centers, revitalized the aura, and charged ourselves with energy. Or at least we should have done it if we have performed the exercises correctly. And this means building meanings into the God-names, actually trying to *feel* the energy as it flows through the body, and in, out and down through the aura.

As in sport, achievement depends upon constant practice and training. A few halfhearted attempts at this exercise will achieve little. Similarly, training in sports implies more than just a few desultory push-ups.

## Gaining New Qualities

This particular exercise can be applied toward practical ends. Sensational writers always promise wondrous effects on the material plane, so we may as well look at the rationale behind this, for there is no doubt that magic can be used to gain things on this level.

Let us suppose that the student has reached a

stage in the practice of this exercise when he can really feel the energies flowing and being directed as he chooses (and he *will* reach this stage). Let us suppose further that he wishes to travel. What he would now do, after completing the Middle Pillar technique is to visualize his aura turning into bright orange, shining with the light of Hod. He would be in the midst of this light, looking out, suffused by the whole glow. As he visualizes this he intones the godname of Elohim Tzavoos as he identifies strongly with the qualities of Mercury and travel, and communication. He wills himself to believe that all the forces of travel in the universe are achieving a sympathetic vibration with him which will lead to his achieving his goal.

Having finished this, the practitioner, as he goes about his daily work, should bend his mind to the thoughts of travel and to the possibilities that might bring it about. He may find that if he starts applying, he will gain a travel scholarship; or he may find a sympathetic relative; or a sum of money may come his way to enable his wish to fulfill itself. If worked on strongly enough and often the aim will indeed manifest itself through ordinary channels, yet with definite impulses from inner levels. But more than this, the magician achieves his effect by putting himself into a frame of mind which is actively attuned to the possibilities and the half-chance. He opens his eyes and his will to areas in his life that he may not have noticed before and makes efforts along these lines.

Alternatively, he may use the same sphere for a job in, say teaching. In this case he would formulate his image of the type of job and proceed in the same way. What he would not do the next day, however, is sit back and wait for an offer to appear miraculously through his letterbox. Like any mortal being he would have to supply the Malkuth qualities by writing applications, looking at the lists of vacancies, and keeping his ears open for any forthcoming posts. When he does finally get the sort of job he wants it may well be because at the interview he was so attuned to the teacher qualities of Hod and Mercury that he was the obvious choice.

Obviously, what this technique enables is for the user to evoke chosen qualities within himself. In less complex ways we can do this by singing songs when we feel inspired, or by dancing, or by countless other means. This exercise, however, consciously aims at evoking certain areas, and with specific intensity. We can use it to make ourselves feel courageous and strong by using Geburah; to make ourselves feel more harmonious through Tiphereth. Yet these qualities are to be regarded as there already, and the exercise as a means of bringing them out and developing them. It is not a question of courage, or whatever, being grafted on from an outside source.

In his excellent essay *The Art of True Healing* (from which this technique is unashamedly stolen), Israel Regardie goes into some detail regarding the practical application of the Middle Pillar exercise. Those interested should refer themselves accordingly.* In all the attempts to gain material benefit through magical means, however, we must bear in mind the old maxim that what we ask for is very often not what we want. Or to quote from W.E. Butler: "Be very careful what you ask for in magic, because you might be unlucky—and get it." It is like the person who desires nothing more than to be rich, and who finds, on achieving his desire, that it is at the cost of family, friendship, and health. If we are to ask for anything at all in magic it should be in the realm of higher qualities, rather than tangible things, for if there is any one law in this universe it seems to be that there is a price to pay for everything.

---

*The essay can be found in Regardie's *Foundations of Practical Magic* (Aquarian Press, 1979).

# 5
# The Banishing and Invoking Ritual

The very glamorous concept of a banishing ritual is no more than an attempt to create, as far as possible, a sterile spiritual atmosphere in and around the operator. It is no more than what a surgeon would do. The magician's aim is to try and simulate the condition of Ain Soph Aur within the place of working. A definite sphere of force is created around the magician in performing this, and even the least psychic of people can feel a real difference in the atmosphere.

What we will briefly analyze here is the classic "Banishing Ritual of the Pentagram." This was a ritual devised within the scheme of the Golden Dawn. It is still regarded by many—if not most—magicians as the standard technique for the particular purpose. But while it is an effective and valuable piece we have to remember that it was created almost a century ago. The

men and women who devised the Golden
Dawn workings were doing so for their own
time. Modern versions of the banishing ritual
often do without the god-forms and pentacles
entirely, using, in one instance, a 3-D version of
the circle-cross. So while we ought to study this
Pentagram ritual in its classic form for the sake
of understanding our magical foundations, and
while it is still a potent and fascinating technique, we must bear in mind the idea that it is
rather dated. However it is given here as means
of introducing the student in a short simple way
to the method and meaning of magic, and because it is almost a summary of all the techniques we have discussed so far.

## The Qabalistic Cross

The first part of the Ritual is the Qabalistic
Cross. This can be used prior to other rituals
than banishing rituals. It is a device for "switching on." It symbolizes the beginning of the rites,
and their dedication to God.

Begin by facing east. This can be geographical east, or mystical east, which is simply in
front of you, no matter the actual direction. This
is where darkness turns Light, presided over by
Raphael who associates with Sephira Hod and
ritual magic.

Bring your arms from your sides out and up
in a wide sweep and down to a spot just above
the forehead (Kether). Your hands should be

palms together as in prayer.

This done, say "To thee God," then bring your hand down to the solar plexus and say "Be the Kingdom"; bring them up to the right shoulder, " ... and the Power"; across to the left shoulder, "And the Glory ... " Then cross your arms against your body and say " ... Unto the Ages of Ages, Amen." As you do this, visualize a beam of brilliance traveling from above the head down to *the feet*, then completing the cross from right to left shoulder.

In this case, we substitute Tiphereth for Malkuth (the Kingdom), because stooping to touch the Malkuth center at the feet would make the actual rite clumsy. Thus Tiphereth becomes a symbolic Malkuth for the purpose of grace and ease.

Those of you who studied the diagram of the Microcosmic Man will realize that the Power and Glory refer to Geburah and Chesed (also called Gedulah) situated at the right and left shoulders. As the beam comes down, visualize the Divine Force coming to Earth, to link Man with God for the performance of this rite. Similarly, visualize the scourging, purifying force of Geburah cleansing the aura, and the steadying forces of Chesed, balancing these forces, and steadying the aura. Finally, visualize the radiant cross and yourself as gigantic, echoing the words across the universe.

These words in Hebrew are "Ateh (*Artay*),

Malkuth, ve Geburah ve Gedulah, le Olahm. Amen."

Some of you may realize that this is not the traditional method; that is, we use both hands, instead of only the first and second fingers of the right hand, as in the more established version. But it is important to develop original ideas. It is important to modify and evolve existing techniques. It does not matter whether they are unsuitable for others, as long as they are suitable for you, then they are valid. Try both variants of the Qabalistic Cross (there are others). See which "feels right" for you. Can you think of any improvements? Try them. They may not be very satisfactory, but they are a step in the right direction.

## Tracing a Five-Pointed Star

Still facing east, trace in the air in front of you a large five-pointed star. Start at the bottom left-hand point of the star. Right hand stretched down across your body, bring it up above and in front of you to create the top point, down and to the right to create the bottom right-hand point. Continue so that the other points are about level with your shoulders, and finish where you started. As your hand travels, visualize the star being formed out of glowing energy coming through the tips of your first and second fingers. So now you have a large, sym-

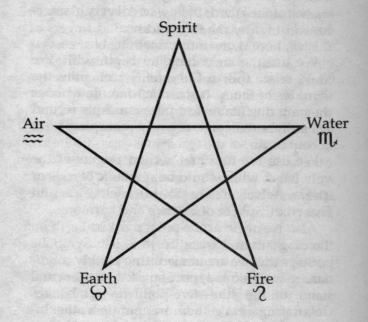

*Figure 3. The Five-Pointed Star*

metrical five-pointed star glowing in the air in front of you, in your imagination. This star is then energized by stabbing the center and uttering one of the Words of Power. All very glamorous—but what is the significance?

Well, here is one interpretation.

We use the right hand to begin with. We could relate this to Geburah, which rules the shoulder of the Microcosmic Man. Remember we are trying to create a pure atmosphere, and Geburah is the constructively scourging force to help us do so.

We use the first and second fingers of the right hand, which could be symbolic of rods or spears, which relate to Michael, Fire and Tiphereth, Sphere of balance and harmony.

Also we begin at the point marked Earth on the diagram and trace up to Spirit. Symbolic perhaps that we are transmuting earthly conditions to conditions of pure spirit. And the actual shape of the star—five-pointed—symbolizes Geburah again. Yet there are countless other interpretations. There is nothing profound about this one. Look for your own and the ritual will gain power.

Having energized the center, turn 90° to your right and do the same again, then twice more until you are facing east again. Now visualize the four great stars surrounding you, glowing, set at the limits of the space available.

## Building the Archangels

We now begin to build the archangels. Turn back and read about them. Remember that constant visualization will "solidify" on astral levels forms which will be ensouled by the corresponding intelligences. These archangels will act as channels for contacting the forces they represent. Being concerned with the creative levels of energy, they also act as mediators of forces which might otherwise be overwhelming.

So, arms outstretched (why?), we visualize Raphael first. Now intone, "Before me Raphael; behind me Gabriel; on my right hand Michael; on my left hand Auriel. For around me flame the pentagram, and above me shines the six-rayed star." As the archangels are mentioned, sense the feelings of Air, Water, Fire and Earth. Picture it as vividly as you can. Dwell upon their characteristics as you name them. There is no hurry. Finally finish the ritual by formulating the Qabalistic Cross again.

If you are not familiar with this ritual, it may seem complicated, but in practice it is much easier than it reads. Of course it would have been simpler for you if the instructions had been tabulated. But in the case of this book, the purpose is not to tell *how* to do the rituals, but rather *why* to do them; or at least get you thinking for yourself. That is why the information is not grouped conveniently in one place.

## Further Aspects

Now you know how to purify a place in preparation for magical work. There is yet another aspect of this ritual, however, which will shed further light on it. With only one variation the method can be used to invoke particular forces. The variation is simply that you begin the star at the point marked "spirit," and trace down to the Earth point, and so on.

In banishing, use the word "Adonai" as you stab the center of the star. As you intone the word, picture yourself as a mighty lord cleansing the Quarter you face by power of command and gesture.

In invoking, the word is chosen according to the Sphere you are dealing with. Thus operations of Venus would use the God-name of Netzach. As you invoke this force you imagine it coming "down" and filling you in answer to your calling. Also, the archangels face *towards* you when invoking, and *away* when banishing.

So now you know how to banish unwanted forces, invoke wanted forces, and circulate force within your aura. Within the variety of these techniques are the bases for the whole of ritual magic. When you come to create your own rituals, you will use these same methods, even though the application will be different.

The lower triad of the Tree—Hod, Netzach, Yesod—gives us a clue to these techniques. In fact it is sometimes known as the "magical triangle." Hod supplies us with the intellectual reasoning behind the ritual; Netzach gives it the flair and sympathy; and Yesod links intellect and emotion to subconscious levels so that the concepts take effect as described before. Malkuth meanwhile supplies the physical basis for ritual.

## Your Own Name

One technique which might be of value in connection with the Banishing Ritual is to repeat your own name to yourself, seeing the letters, and hearing your voice booming across the universe and echoing back to you. Imagine that the whole of your life-force is in that name. Now cut off the last letter of the name but keep on intoning it within your mind. Now another letter and another, and as each letter is omitted feel your personality fading, feel your whole self dissolving until the final letter of your name is gone and you are just Void and Nothingness. This is another and sonic attempt to achieve some semblance of the quality of Ain Soph Aur within. Use it to reinforce and supplement the Banishing Ritual if necessary. The medieval charm based on the word *Abracadabra* is related to this aim. By identifying an illness with the word, then reducing the letters in the word, the illness was supposed to fade accordingly.

ABRACADABRA
ABRACADABR
ABRACADAB
ABRACADA
ABRACAD
ABRACA
ABRAC
ABRA
ABR
AB
A

And after this we would emphasize the need to return to normal consciousness by a reversal of these techniques.

# 6
# Astral Magic

The technique we will study now is one relying entirely upon the imaginative faculty, without the support of any ritual gestures.

Essentially it involves the creation of forms in the Astral Light which are used as vehicles for the Inner Intelligences they are aimed at. These forms are also known as "telesmatic images."

This system of working is generally known as Astral Magic. It belongs to the realm of Yesod, sometimes called "The Treasure House of Image."

In some cases, the method involves visualizing yourself as a particular character in a symbolic mental drama, the aim being to evoke the qualities and experiences of that character in yourself.

You may well question the validity of this system. The obvious criticism is that the user will be living in a dream fantasy land, a self-induced fairy-tale.

This is true of course if the user forgets the correct approach to symbolism—the approach we have stressed throughout the book. We are assuming, however, that the user is a competent magician, using a controlled symbol-system, aware that the images are his *own* creation.

Even so, where is the psychology behind this? Where is the contact with everyday life?

In answer, turn back to our earlier definition of magic as a means of growing up.

## Hero Figures

At various stages of life, we all have the need of myth and hero figures. The are necessary. They supply us with symbols of aspiration. They show us something of the standards we should try to achieve.

In very young children, the hero figures are their parents, whom they copy and identify with in their games. Later, they graduate through traditional folk-heroes to contemporary ones. In each case, the children hope to be able to recreate the experiences and attitudes of these figures within themselves.

Some of these we outgrow, like Santa Claus and Robin Hood; others we continually aspire to, particularly in the fields of religion and sport.

This is why the family is so important. If the parents supply the appropriate hero qualities, the child will benefit. Unfortunately, this is not always the case. Often, the child has to find his own hero figures. For example, a child lacking in paternal influences may choose a figure expressing manliness and virility. Hopefully he does not choose to copy the local thug.

We outgrow these images when we have absorbed the qualities built into them by our imagination. It is simply a matter of identity-seeking, which is a step on the way to fulfilling the maxim of "Man—Know Thyself."

All this is in the realm of Yesod, the plane of Illusion. Think back to the times of your first love. Think how that person seemed to be the most perfect creature alive, yet how the illusion faded slightly if not completely with time. We build up images around things which either fade with our own increasing maturity, or remain because their qualities are still above our own immediate potential.

Yesod is concerned very much with the formative years of puberty, when the need for myth figures is great. But the lesson of Yesod is one of independence on all planes in all ways. As more and more of the Yesod-ic qualities are absorbed, the dependence on heroic and father-mother figures becomes less and less. It is a process of seeing through the glamour of things which obscures the true essence. Much of the hideous glamour of magic is there because we have put it there ourselves, and one of the purposes of this book is to strip some of this glamour away.

Although this is an apparent digression from Astral Magic, it is important that we understand the psychology of every day behind it, for how else can magic work?

## Background Ideas

Remember it is not the images themselves that are important, but the forces or collective experiences behind them. The mental psychodramas involve archetypal symbols and characters taking part in situations beyond our normal experiences. We try to absorb some of these experiences, or rather, bring out of ourselves the qualities we are looking for, using carefully chosen symbols which will link with inner actualities.

Changing ideas about the symbols will show up as changes in the symbols themselves. Great concentration is needed, for it is useless to rush through the working. You must take it slowly, examining and analyzing each step, each symbol, building new concepts into them. As the concepts develop, the symbols will gain in power.

Essentially, Astral Magic is meditation materialized to visual imagery. Some find this more palatable than the meditative analysis of abstract concepts, but we must think about this. Many people take to this way of working because the relative austerities of mysticism become dull and boring.

## A Working

However, let us look at a typical piece of working and then analyze it.

Sit or lie comfortably, breathing calmly and steadily. Empty your mind of all extraneous thoughts and images.

The journey begins from a beach—not an ordinary beach, but one with sand of citrine and olive colors.

You are lying on this beach, a few yards from the sea, with the beach itself stretching away behind you to infinity. The sun burns down, but its rays do not tan. Instead they inflame you with a desire to trap the rays at their source and absorb them within the innermost recesses of your being. You reach out to catch them, to touch the sun which seems so huge and near, but you fail and sink back on the sand.

Beneath you feel the earth, firm and solid and massive, with you as a mere speck upon the surface. It offers firm and solid comfort, far more than that distant sun. Even so ...

But you are drawn away from these thoughts by the sense of the sea so near to you. Sitting up, you look across its waves of surging violet. Suddenly, the whole surface is disturbed by a mighty figure, a classical Neptune, rising out of the sea. Laughingly he raises a silver cup filled with sparkling liquid, and offers it to you, then sinks invitingly back into the sea before you can accept.

Deeply moved by this awesome, god-like figure, you pace the nine steps down to the surf and wade in, and as you do so, you melt *into* the sea: you *become* the sea and feel its currents and tides as your own.

For a seeming eternity you stay in that state completely at one with the sea, but gradually, persistently, there comes a beckoning call from above.

The caller is Michael, clad in his robes of fire and pointing at you with his spear. Seeing the kindly wisdom in his eyes, you remember your original urge, and call out to him with all the force of your spiritual yearning.

You re-organize into a compact entity. No longer are you the sea; it is time to reach further.

Gripping the butt-end of the spear which is offered to you, you pull yourself up to face Michael. Immediately behind him is a colossal sun within easy reach in but a few steps. Michael smiles at the fear and hesitation you show, but taking you gently by the shoulder, he leads you towards that sun. As you get nearer, you realize that it emanates spiritual intensity rather than physical heat, and the rays engulf you, blotting out everything but the swirling golden clouds flecked with rose and salmon colors, which stream and shape into a whirl-pool.

You cannot see Michael now, but you sense his presence nearby. All you are aware of is being sucked into that vortex, and thrown out on to firm ground again.

The worst is over, and as you look around, you feel a confidence and inspiration that you have never known before, you feel that you are on the fringe of a known but long-forgotten land. The colors of fire, the flame-shaped mountains in the distance, all conspire to set alight something inside you. But your immediate concern is the road that you are standing on, a broad road leading to a building in the distance, and straddled by a huge golden hexagram. Michael is back by this time, and he gives you a push in the small of your back to set you out towards that place. As you step through the hexagram you feel like a lizard that has lost his old skin—lighter, happier. Close to the building now, you pause at the bottom of the six large and high steps leading up to the doorway ...

On either side of the doorway is a lion, growling. But remember that you have come a long way, gone through some strange and new experiences, and to turn back at this stage would be the action of an undedicated coward. Now you walk a sure and steady line between the lions which you find are not as big as they had seemed at a distance, and certainly not as frightening.

The inner chamber now. Six-sided, with an

altar in the middle large enough to take a person lying down. And so you do so ...

Now invoke the spirit of whatever sun-contact you want to make, using whatever system you use, be He Apollo, Osiris, Michael, Christ or Whoever. For the purposes of this working which is essentially Qabalistic, let us use Michael. Realize that the person who has been leading you was just an earthly image of you own creation, ensouled by a partial essence of your own Michael-ic qualities leading you here. Now that you have raised your consciousness nearer to that of the Source, invoke Michael himself that He may enfold some of the Tiphereth qualities within you.

Whatever it is that you want to achieve, visualize it; see yourself in the future as you want to be in relation to the qualities you are aiming for. Or perhaps you want some answer to a question that is concerned with the affairs of Tiphereth. If so, then ask it. Do not expect some booming voice to answer, however. Rather look for some quiet realization in the near future.

The important thing now is to retrace your steps exactly the way you came. You have just raised your consciousness somewhat (how far depends upon experience), and now you must return to normal levels, so go through the stages of your journey in reverse, until you end up at the beach again.

**Analyzing the Working**

As stated, there is no reason why this cannot be adapted to Pagan practice. The hexagram is a universal symbol of opposites in perfect balance: Fire and Water, Male and Female, Positive and Negative. It is a symbol of us all as we cope with the good and bad, the bright and dark, the lucky and the unlucky aspects within us. Tiphereth is the realm of the Sun, that sphere which holds all things in its orbit, and which itself is comprised of colossal, opposing energies held in perfect balance. Whatever God or Goddess the magician may identify as being central or radiant to his cult, can be used with or without the six-pointed star. Working along these lines, in this direction, means that the magician will be entering areas of individual and collective experience in which the principle of "Willing Sacrifice" occurs.

In a simple way readers can make a start at contacting the essence behind each of the spheres by asking themselves a series of simple questions:

*Malkuth:* Have I ever asked why am I here? What am I doing?

*Yesod:* Have I ever had intense, evocative dreams?

*Hod:* Have I ever gained satisfaction from using my intellect?

*Netzach:* Have I ever known moments of great passion and romance?

*Tiphereth:* Have I ever willingly sacrificed anything for the sake of others (e.g. sacrificing a career for the sake of children)?

*Geburah:* Have I ever made a stern but absolutely impartial decision on any situation?

*Chesed:* Have I ever been generous for the sake of being generous?

*Binah:* Have I ever known great sorrow, which has brought understanding?

*Chockmah:* Have I ever known a great surging of joy in which all things seemed possible?

*Kether:* Have I ever known the still, small voice within?

These and other questions can literally be asked of yourself, and those experiences which form the answers remembered as intensely as possible. It is as if certain groupings of brain cells were being explored in sequence, and activated in varying ways at varying levels. The more we can relate every aspect of our own lives to the groupings or Spheres in question, the greater potential we have for illuminating ourselves. Symbols such as the hexagram then become a means of tuning into the energies we seek.

As with everything else, these very simple questions are purely examples. We can and should ask ourselves many others. The magical techniques using the visualized journey and specific symbols are integral to this process. They are often means of formulating questions and receiving answers before we are *consciously* aware of having asked. Using them all together, we can create a battering ram which can smash though barriers in the mind.

Although we began in this instance by starting from a beach, many of these workings begin from a temple, the direction of exit being governed by the type of working. Some of the preliminary exercises in magical training involve the creation of an inner temple. It is the astral temple created by a trained imagination which is most important, rather than the physical, outer temple. It is the astral equivalents of the magical weapons which actually give them their force, linked as they are with the subconscious mind. The principle is quite readily found in lovers' keepsakes: to anyone else they may be items of junk; to the lovers concerned they are treasures indeed, which can retain a curious power of enchantment for the rest of one's life. It is the memories, associations, and subconscious links which thus give the items their power. This is why you must visualize the temple or weapons or whatever, embodying the concepts you want. Take modern advertisements which read something like: "How to be a real man, and prove irresistible to women!" In most cases the secret is in imagining yourself as a smooth, suave charmer and repeating that well-known phrase which suggests: "Hour by hour, day by day, I'm more attractive in every way." The ideas here are much the same, being aimed at bringing out certain qualities by means of the controlled imagination.

## Visualizing a Temple

So let us now begin to visualize a temple, build it piece by piece, and set it firmly in the astral levels of our minds. Let it be in whatever outward shape which appeals to you—a castle, a cottage, or something in the Grecian style—but it is wiser in the early stages to keep it as simple as possible. Inside it should be a four-walled affair to correspond with the Elements. It is going to be the starting point for the magical workings, so the floor tiles might be colored according to the scheme of Malkuth. The walls might possibly be hung with tapestries depicting the Man, Lion, Bull and Eagle of Aquarius, Leo, Taurus and Scorpio. The altar could be a double cube of black and white upon which is laid the magical weapons, covered by a silk cloth.

These are the general details, the rest you must imagine for yourself, for it is you who will be working in it, no one else. Visualize the scene strongly and regularly, beginning from here with your Astral Magic, leaving by a hidden door behind the appropriate tapestry and returning by the same.

Over a period of time you will come to alter the shape and style of this astral temple as you would a real house. Eventually it will fix itself firmly within your mind. Perhaps we might think of it in terms of Jung's tower at Bollingen. Here is a place we go to when we want to shut out the mundane and trivial and attempt to commune with our deepest selves. We must especially learn to visualize the approach and entrance-way to this temple. The opening of this door should be a deliberate signal to shrug off the last vestiges of the petty and the mundane, and leave outside anything which is inconsistent with the concept of this as a temple.

At one level what we are doing is creating at least one place within our world where everything is peaceful, secure, and devoid of the crassness of the outer world. This is why time and concern should be devoted to building up this image. It is, after all, a temple, holy place and sanctuary, where can be found the qualities of spiritual stimulus, warmth, nourishment, and security.

Aleister Crowley, in his trek across China, realized that due to the relative nature of time *and* space, he could actually bring his temple in Scotland to him, so to speak. Of course he meant the astral equivalent of the physical temple, in which he could perform just as effectively. When we talk about something being on the astral plane, however, we are simply saying that it is in the unconscious mind. So the inner temple—no matter how simple—is all that we need to work from, even if it is at present impossible to set aside an actual room for the purpose.

While on these lines, here is another example of visualizing which may be useful.

Begin in your temple, standing next to the altar facing east. Now imagine yourself growing, quickly and steadily, growing far above the temple which is at your feet somewhere below, seeing the curvature of the earth become a full circle as the whole globe beneath you. See the stars coming closer as you grow ever bigger, see the earth disappear completely, feel yourself absorb suns, planets and galaxies, until there is nothing else to absorb and you stand supreme as the Heavenly Man himself. What do you feel now? What are the implications of this? What practical purpose could this exercise have?

These questions you have to answer for yourself, as no two persons' reactions are the same for any given stimulus.

Of course there is no reason at all why you should not combine these techniques with some of the ritual methods or Middle Pillar exercises, and your own ingenuity will tell you how.

## The Magical Personality

We mentioned earlier the use and value of hero figures and god-forms, and detailed the characteristics of the four major Elemental figures. What we must consider now is the creation of our own magical personality.

It is obvious that while we contain the whole of the Tree within ourselves, nevertheless by virtue of our individuality we tend to gravitate toward one Sphere, or one Element. In the early stages of study efforts must be made to gain an understanding—a *connection*—with all the Spheres, but there comes a point when the mature student will inevitably, almost imperceptibly, find himself specializing in one particular area.

Something of this is hinted in the "Grades" within magic, from Neophyte up to Ipsissimus, taking in all the varieties of Adeptship on the way. Nowadays the idea of vertical progress is very much outmoded, and rightly so, but it does give us the idea that we can cleave to a particular Sphere. Thus in the old system an Adeptus Major would be a specialist in the Sphere of Geburah; that is, his psyche is such that it purely expresses the uncompromising qualities of Justice, severity, and courage. On the other hand, someone else may tend to exemplify and channel the qualities of Venus. But the latter is in no wise inferior in spiritual status. Thus a "priest" of the Moon is every bit as potent as a "priest" of Jupiter, but in differing ways.

It is an obvious point, perhaps, but one well worth emphasizing.

What we must eventually determine is our precise area of specialization. Usually it will be quite obvious: after all, to be reading so far in a book on magic in the first place indicates at least some self-awareness. But whether it is obvious or not, the following is a useful exercise.

## Magic Mirror

This involves no more than examining yourself in the light of each Sphere and determining how you measure up. Get a good book on astrology and see how each planet functions and malfunctions within yourself. Supplement this with readings on the Spheres of the Qabalah itself. Brutal honesty is required. There is no earthly use in trying to glamorize yourself to yourself. It can be a salutatory experience to see just how lacking we are in areas we had not even dreamt of before. It can be rather like having some utterly disinterested authority figure giving us a long and blistering list of our faults.

After this, regular returns to this "magic mirror" can help reinforce our attempts to progress toward greater wholeness, and prevent complacency. It is also a means of combating the peculiar smugness that is inherent in many occultists, who mistake this attitude for one of superior wisdom.

However, assuming that the student has built some secure foundations and is quite certain of his own Sphere, what must he do now?

He must conceive of the very highest qualities of Self-hood to which he would aspire. Again, there ought to be nothing petty within this conception, nothing banal. He must determine the type of person he wills to be and in his meditations try to *feel* some of these qualities; he ought to create internal scenes whereby he manifests these qualities in various fields of action.

This is the first step, but one which will carry on over an entire lifetime as his insight and aspirations expand.

The second step is to create the vehicles which will contain this vast cloud of concepts.

This is, in magic, the rather nice term "Body of Light," which generally refers to the astral body but which we can adapt to mean the self-image of the magician operating at his deepest levels of consciousness.

The student then, must determine which Sphere is most akin to himself. In most cases of course one of the Paths would be more appropriate, but in the early days the relatively clear-cut Spheres are easier to use. Let us assume then, that the Sphere of Yesod is chosen.

Somehow, from the mass of lunar symbolism, a design must be chosen. Let us imagine that the magician sees himself in silver-violet robes, adorned with lunar images, a head-band with a crescent symbol set on his brow, and with a cowl, perhaps. He sees himself dressed like this. If he is unhappy with his everyday physical shape then he can alter it in his imagination into what he deems appropriate. When in his imagination he is adorned thus, he exemplifies all of the highest qualities of the Moon he has been studying and sensing for years. The assumption of this image (or god-form, if you like) is the signal to assume those greater-than-normal qualities. He becomes a Priest of the Moon indeed, functioning more closely towards his true Self. But only for the duration of the rite.

In time, when the student has some surer visualization of the images, he may come to make his own robes to match these inner ones, but at present it is still early stages.

## Magical Names

We mentioned earlier the use and value of the "Names of Power" connected with each Sphere. One of the tasks of the magician is to create his own Magical Name which will sum up the qualities toward which he aspires. In the first stages of study we can simply use the god-name of a Sphere, but when shades and subtleties become apparent to the inward gaze, we have to find some Name to summarize them. It is common knowledge that the pen name of the

English occultist Dion Fortune was derived from her motto "Deo non Fortuna"; W.B. Yeats' Magical Name (or Motto) was "Demon est Deus Inversus," or D.E.D.I. as he would sign himself; Aleister Crowley began as "Perdurabo" ("I Will Endure unto the End") and developed to "To Mega Therion," the Great Beast.

Now our own Names do not need to be in Latin, Greek, or anything else beyond our ken. They do not have to take the form of mottoes, either. Any invented word which somehow sums up what you feel to express your highest Self will do. What is important is that you do not publicize the Name; that you tell no one— no matter how close they are. It is to become your one secret, your ultimate Mystery. It will express *who* you are. When the Name is found it will provide one of the most important of all the keys to invoking and controlling very great levels of energy indeed. We should spend time throwing together combinations of words and syllables even though the early results will inevitably sound weak—not to say silly. However, as is the way with magic, the right name for the moment will eventually assert itself. It will feel right. It may change over the years but so do we all. It is up to us to initiate the process.

### Switching Off

So now we have a whole range of techniques whereby we can slip out of our mundane consciousness and key ourselves into a magical personality that can project us into new realms of experience. We must always be careful however, to make deliberate efforts to "switch off" when the workings are over. This shifting of gear is a common enough occurrence in everyday life. The man who dominates his subordinates at work and yet who is submissive at home is simply exercising different aspects of his nature. There should be situations in all of our lives whereby we can use several gears, otherwise we would end up straining the engines. Ritual and the Magical Personality provide the extra gear and the broad road to be able to cruise with ease at high speeds for a while.

# 7
# The Tarot and the Tree of Life

One of the most important aspects of the Western Magical Tradition is the Tarot deck, and its relationship to the paths on the Tree of Life.

The origins of the pack are unimportant. Whether they are from ancient Egypt or medieval Europe does not matter. The fact is that they provide us with a wealth of profound imagery which we can use to push even further inward.

The deck itself is split into two portions: the Major Arcana, consisting of 22 cards, and the Minor Arcana, consisting of 56 cards divided into four suits which parallel those of the playing cards we know today.

Now whether by accident or design the cards of the Major Arcana seem tailor-made for the 22 paths on the Tree, but it is here that generations of students have become ensnared by attempts to find the "true" system of attribution. However, we hope by now that it is apparent there is no such thing. The images of the Tarot are there for the individual to interpret for himself and thus gain a measure of real affinity with them. Likewise, it is a test of his own perception for him to be able to place the cards upon the Tree according to his understanding of both. It is quite irrelevant that Crowley or Waite or Fortune might have written something about a particular card if you yourself suspect a completely different interpretation. Adhere to your own analysis—but keep a flexible attitude.

There are of course many varieties of Tarot decks. Perhaps too many if the truth were known. Some, such as the Robin Wood Tarot, and the Reed/Cannon Witches Tarot, plus the New Golden Dawn Ritual Tarot are excellent. Some would have been better off saving a few trees by never being published at all. But for our present purposes we will use the images of the Waite/Rider version.

A.E. Waite, even taking into account the era in which he wrote, must rank as one of the most excruciatingly boring and obfuscated of all the occult writers. Yet somehow, in collaboration with Pamela Colman Smith, he has presented us with a truly extraordinary symbol-system for use in the Qabalistic scheme.

The deck on its own, though, is rather like having a road map in thick fog which will only become useful when some landmarks can be found to enable us to orient ourselves. The landmarks in this case being the Spheres on the Tree.

This is the value in making the effort to align the cards with the various paths; it will give a very definite sense of direction and new impetus.

The paths, as we might imagine, are important in themselves. Crudely put, the areas in which the qualities of the Spheres meet and mingle. Thus the path between Yesod and Netzach is, very basically, that area within our psyche where instincts and emotions are blended. This in itself our course says nothing, which is why a visual symbol at this point becomes of enormous value in helping us to focus.

Fortunately no two students agree as to which of the major cards ought to fit on which path; or if they do agree on this then they disagree on the interpretation. Which is as it should be. It reminds us that there is no dogma within the magical tradition.

In the past century the most usual way to attribute the cards had been simply to equate the first card with the first path and so on down the ladder, pushing the card known as "The Fool" in at the end. Or else "The Fool," zero, would be related to the first path and the Major Arcana would follow on from that. Undoubtedly these methods have yielded some valuable information but, I feel, they have limited themselves by feeling obliged to retain the numerical sequence of the deck.

Of all the differing arrangements the one that

seems most reasonable is that given by W.G. Gray in his brilliant book *Magical Ritual Methods*.

As we can see from Figure 4, the deck appears to fall naturally into terms of positive, negative and neutral, as does the Tree itself. Starting with the Middle Pillar we not a progression from Malkuth to Kether by way of Moon, Sun, and Star. If nothing else, these cards actually relate to the correct planetary Spheres, which they do not in many of the other systems. Interestingly enough, the progression of religious worship often takes just such a path: from the lunar and matriarchal systems of the Celts, for example, changing gradually to the solar and patriarchal systems as Christianity was introduced; leading to the intense and purely individual stellar consciousness within ourselves. Or perhaps to some stellar religion which may be forthcoming in the Aquarian Age.

On the left-hand or negative pillar we can see cards like "The Devil," "Death," "The Hanged Man," and "The Tower," while the positive side of the Tree contains "The Empress," "Temperance," "Strength," "The Emperor"—all essentially beneficent and secure images.

The three horizontal paths equate with different levels of fate, or free-will: "The Wheel of Fortune" being pure random chance events arising from the qualities of reason or romance

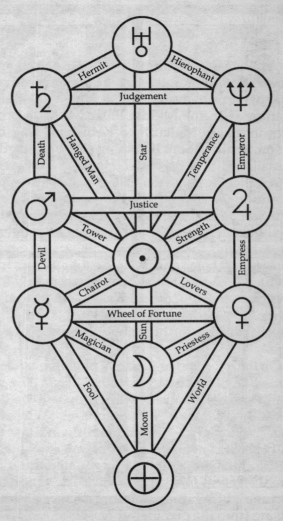

*Figure 4.*

*Figure 5.*

*Figure 6.*

and the whims of both; "Justice" which is more purely karma, and which connects with our ethical sense as well; and "Judgement" which is our own assessment of our life in the light of mature wisdom and understanding—such as is said to occur as part of the after-death experience.

At the very bottom of the Tree we see "The World" and "The Fool," symbolic of unindividuated humanity of two different types, while just above them are symbols of what we have been talking about throughout this whole book: "The Magician" and "The Priestess." They are both linked with Yesod, and remember that it is through connection with the unconscious that magic works. In the former we have the purely Hermetic type, while in the latter we have the Orphic. Even a cursory glance at the "High Priestess" with its symbols of sea, moon, and sexuality shows it to be an especially relevant attribution.

But not, in any sense, the *correct* one. Only you can find that.

With "The Lovers" we can see something of the mechanics of love, and it is a wonder why, with the huge solar image of Michael above them, no one has sought fit to put this card in this position before. While opposite, in "The Chariot," is the sort of person whose intellect is such that he develops an acute insight into the world at large even though he himself rarely goes out into it, and is fastened into one place as the charioteer of this card is fastened into a cubic stone. The Philosopher's Stone, perhaps.

The image of the lightning-struck "Tower" connecting Tiphereth and Geburah is obvious, while we can see both solar and jovian symbols within the card known as "Strength."

"The Hanged Man" and "Temperance" at the supernal levels on the Tree show different ways toward wisdom and understanding, while at the very top "The Hermit" and "The Hierophant" show different ways to express these qualities for the benefit of those souls struggling up after them.

It is impossible to go into any depth about individual cards and paths here; but just to show, however, how well the Waite Tarot deck fits into the scheme, let us take a brief look at just one of the cards and its path.

## The Hermit

This is the ninth card of the Major Arcana. It features a tall patriarch in robes of dark gray or black, standing on a mountain top. His face is in profile, he holds a lantern in his right hand and a staff in his left. In the distance are other snow-covered peaks.

We must note that in Gray's system of attributions this card is placed on the path between Kether and Binah. We might note that he shares the same colors as the latter Sphere, and is a creature of Silence, which is also one of the titles of Binah. His face is remarkably like the Magical Image of Kether—a bearded king, seen in profile—while the mountain-top symbolism reminds us that we are indeed dealing with consciousness at supernal levels. Taking the hermit's staff as the center-line, if we equate this with the Middle Pillar, then we can see that the lantern is being held at the Binah position. We might decide that he is looking down at struggling humanity and lightning the way for them. Unlike his counterpart "The Hierophant" or Master Magician, he leads by example rather than by precept.

At this point the student should also apply a similar approach to the position of "The Hierophant" and determine how the two complement and balance each other, working down the whole Tree in the same way. Ignore the usual divinatory meanings given to each card and simply regard each image as a new piece of art to be interpreted in the light of certain principles. In the early efforts it may seem that very little of original value is forthcoming, but as the student gets increasingly familiar with both Tarot and Tree it will come to feel as though a dam is beginning to burst.

In this way each card will begin to "come alive" within the psyche, broadening the limits of awareness. This is all that is meant when occultists talk about imprinting the Tarot or the

Tree within the aura. It is not, as might be imagined, a case of magicians going about as though they had fairy-lights within their auras, festooned like Christmas trees; rather does it mean that these arcane glyphs have rooted into the unconscious simply because their user has worked hard at putting them there. We see again the lower Spheres in action within this process: Malkuth, the physical process involved in the student sitting down with pen and paper to analyze the glyphs; Netzach, the desire and imagination providing the impulse; intellect and all the processes needed for interpretation coming from Hod; while Yesod is the bowl of the unconscious—the powerhouse— which will store all the data for future use.

## Tarot Magic

When the student gets tired from this considerable effort he can choose an exotic diversion to get him over the dry patch. This involves one of the visualization techniques whereby a Tarot card is imagined as a living scene into which it is possible to step. You might find yourself "inside" the card of "The Chariot." You will talk to the charioteer and ask him why he is embedded in stone, what is the significance of the black and white sphinxes, and of the canopy above him. Even if there is no apparent result or else nothing more than a fanciful response from your own imagination, it is still a means of becoming so thoroughly acquainted with the images that you become like best friends, gradually giving and receiving thoughts that could never come from strangers.

We could begin with the Tarot card "The Moon." After all the preliminary clearing and tuning techniques have been done and the astral temple created, we find ourselves looking into the scene of that card, and determining to explore that path which leads from Malkuth to Yesod. In our magical form we find ourselves facing the pylon gate in a twilight land, with wild beasts howling at either side of us. What, we ask ourselves, is taking place behind those square windows high up in each tower? What is the significance of the tears that the lunar orb seems to be shedding? What will we find at the end of this rough road when we get beyond the distant peaks? We must then visualize ourselves as actually walking along this path, keeping a lookout for the denizens of the world around. Images will arise. Nonsensical ones perhaps, but interesting nonetheless. When we finally crest the peaks depicted in this card we will see, perhaps, a Moon Temple, surrounded by nine maidens and Mysteries taking place within. The task is then to seek admittance to this place (Yesod) and see what else we may learn.

At the end, no matter how little we may feel that we have achieved, we must retrace our steps until we find ourselves back in our own little astral temple and ready to step back into Malkuth again.

It is an interesting technique and one which can yield surprising results in time, but it must be emphasized that it is, by and large, a diversion. The real work can only be done through mental sweat and conscious study of each card. No matter how splendid the visions that may arise during any astral magical exercises, unless the student can relate these to fundamental concepts and experiences within his mundane world then he will find them of no earthly use. Inducing visions is easy. The hard thing is to induce wisdom.

## Divination

Using the cards for this purpose is an excellent way to learn more about them. The important thing in this process is not in being able to predict the future but in learning how the cards can relate to each other, and modify each other.

Most students are advised to use the famed "Ancient Celtic Method" of divination which is given with virtually every deck. In truth the method is neither particularly ancient nor especially Celtic. It is not even very clear.

Also, it is extraordinarily hard to do a divination for yourself. For other people—particularly unhappy people with a real and pressing need for some glimpses of the road ahead—the

Tarot deck can come alive, as any reader will know. The messages behind the glyphs will spring out almost unbidden. For yourself, in a similar state, the spread often does no more than give expression to your gravest, most pessimistic fears.

Magically, while we may occasionally be able to foresee forthcoming events with surprising clarity and accuracy, there comes a point when we actually *create* that future which lies much further ahead. That is, we do not so much glimpse it as make it happen. This is Magic in its highest sense.

We should actually begin with a spread for ourselves, though, no matter how difficult this may be to interpret. After shuffling the deck and cutting it in whatever manner seems appropriate, with either hand, we can place the first ten cards in the positions of the Spheres, starting with Malkuth and working upward.

This, we must realize, offers a pictorial representation of our character and psyche *at this moment of time*. By analyzing each card in the light of each Sphere, we undergo a very real kind of psychoanalysis. This may be appallingly difficult at first, if we are still in the stage of "Gee, who *am* I?" but it gets easier (and often more unpleasant) as we get to know ourselves more. Don't approach the deck in the hope of flattery.

The Spheres can be crudely categorized as:

10. Environment.

9. Instinctual drives and dreams.

8. Mental life and/or occupation.

7. Emotional life.

6. That which is central to the querent's life.

5. That which will come to affect it. Karmic balances.

4. Home and security.

3. Greatest worries.

2. Greatest hopes.

1. What the querent can hope for.

It is like the Rorschach ink-blot test. What do *you* see? If, say, The Hanged Man appears in the Sphere of Venus, what possible message can this hold? In what way can this be symbolic of your love life? Are you being turned upside-down because of some great passion, perhaps? Or if there is no great passion in your life at all, perhaps you need to overturn a possible selfish and unattractive personality in order to develop the radiance and insight that might attract a mate? You have to decide for yourself. Ignore the instruction booklets. Decide for yourself, always.

No one should get too obsessive about this

kind of self-analysis however. Working at it hard and consistently and with exquisite self-honesty is one thing. Becoming obsessional is another.

As stated, when you do a spread for yourself the cards will often say the very last things you might want to hear. But as a new-born magician you must never be afraid to challenge them, and thus challenge Fate itself. This is one of the classic ways to wisdom, after all.

You could actually identify your ideal spread and deliberately place the cards in the pattern of the Tree, putting whichever you would most want to appear in the appropriate Sphere. The spread which then presents itself before you represents the person you most want to be. Calling up your god-figure again you can affirm: "In the name of (N) this is what I will to be," while visualizing these images in your aura. In time, with effort and will, you will grow into them. By then, you will have decided that the next phase of personal growth will use some completely different images.

A fast, very simple method of using the cards is to cut the deck first thing in the morning and ask of it: "Show me a card which might symbolize the day ahead." At the end of the day, after analyzing the events in light of that single card, you can then ask "Now show me the card which will symbolize the lessons I have to learn from today." Speak to the deck out loud. Treat it as a conscious entity. Play games with it.

Another very simple technique is to choose one card to represent yourself, often known as the Significator. Usually you would choose from one of the Court Cards: a King or Queen for an older person, a Knight or Page/Princess for someone younger. However there is nothing wrong with a little bit of arrogance, once in a while, so it might be easier to choose something from the Major Arcana.

While holding the Significator, then, and brooding over a particular problem which is causing you concern, you can shuffle the deck, insert the Significator, and shuffle it again. In a sense, you are sending the card out like a detective whose job it is to track down the true source of your worries. All you do then is simply cut the pack and see what card appears. This, you will understand, will hold a symbolic answer to the question.

Using the cards in conjunction with the Tree is like an astrologer determining what effect a planet will have in any given House. However there is no standard method for Qabalistic divination. Nor should there be for *any* method of divination. It is all a matter of how the individual relates to the energies within him, using symbols that provide a direct route to the subconscious mind. There is nothing easy about it, no way of avoiding hard work.

Quite simply, magical understanding is like

the starlight in The Hermit's lantern. If you want it, there is a long, lonely and bitter climb to reach it, and there are no shortcuts. Remember that the long correspondence tables of organizations like The Order of the Golden Dawn and the rest were composed by ordinary people as capable of erratic thinking, and filled to the brim with as many personal quirks and idiosyncrasies as the rest of us.

You must never be in awe of self-styled adepts and spiritual teachers. If they demand awe from you, then they are not worth bothering with. As regards the use of the Qabalah and the practical methods of application, there is actually so much magical lumber lying around these days that we can do no better than make a clean sweep at the very beginning of things. Return to Ain Soph Aur. Get back to Nothingness. Start with the very basic images of the Tree and circle-cross and build up from there. Say to yourself: "I am what I am—and my magic will be a reflection of this."

It is not easy, but it is the best way of all.

# 8
# Mythological Magic

In an age when so many people are desperate to find their roots and validate themselves either by tracking back their genealogy or else by chasing after their past lives, it is vital that we get back to our spiritual sources. Much, if not all, of Jung's work showed how important it was for every man to have his own myth and to live it out. In the same way we must come to do the same with the ancient images of those mythologies which strike the greatest chords within. It is hardly surprising that people are beginning to do just that, for as Jung said "Everything old is a sign of something coming." The current renaissance of myth and myth-based fantasy, such as deluges the bookstands these days, is a sign of the changing consciousness of our times.

In magic, as we have seen, many of the major images or archetypes are drawn from the Judaeo-Christian tradition which dominates

our Western heritage. Yet the fact is that to
young minds the idea of archangels and the like
is not especially sympathetic and is even quite
embarrassing—even when that person understands the purely symbolic nature of these.
Now although there are sound psychological
reasons why we ought not ignore these old images (and indeed why we *ought* to begin our
training with them) we might at some point
come to consider the use of images from more
appealing sources closer home. As a young
man scrutinizing A.E. Waite's ponderous text, I
could not have imagined using anything other
than Judaeo-Christian imagery. As I move with
reasonable grace into middle age, I relish my
Paganism.

Every race and country has its own mythology, of course, which is often linked to the
"spirit of place" and the actual soil. The mythologies and spiritual practices of the Native
Americans, for example, were not so very far removed from what was practiced in pre-Druidic
times in Western Europe, but modified by land-
scape and climate. Just as the history of a nation
can be described in terms of successive inva-
sions by different peoples, over long periods of
time, so can the mythologies of each·be regarded as akin to rock strata. Some magicians,
then, are quite happy with the Judaeo-Christian
surface on which they stand, in the dust of
which they inscribe their Circles of Art. Others

are constantly impelled to dig deeper. Yet all the levels support, nourish, or give drainage to the others, if the truth were known. The Pagan, Wiccan heritage is in no way inferior to the Christian, and vice-versa. While at the end of the day, or the beginning of the eon, it will be the new upsurge of the Native American tradition which will provide the generations to come with the soaring heights they will need; while the religious and mythological topsoil of the present, will sink down to become the bedrock of the future.

Americans, in fact, are in a unique position. As shown in my book *Earth God Rising*, ancient impulses figure just as much in the national life of the New World as they ever did in the witch-haunted lands of the Old. Presidents Lincoln and Kennedy, for instance, provide clear modern parallels to the Pagan exemplars of the Divine King and Sacrificed God. And even numinous, charismatic figures from the world of rock music and the movies can be seen as manifestations of inner energies relevant to us all. In Europe these energies are often summoned and stirred from the remote past and brought forward into the present by various occult groups of both Pagan and Christian inclinations. In America similar energies sparkle in the present and have the potential for opening up the future. If this seems paradoxical at the moment, then it will become clear the moment that the individual makes links with such imagery.

That which occurred over thousands of years in Europe and elsewhere, often comes to the boil within a few generations in America. There is an old Celtic myth about the bubbling cauldron of the Goddess, which can give a person all knowledge if they can just drink from it. America, the melting pot, can be regarded by its inhabitants as just such a cauldron. It is up to the individual to stand on tiptoes and peer over the brim, into the bubbling contents, and use the ladles of choice and whim to scoop out whatever seems most nourishing.

There is no reason, therefore, why a modern American may not work the magic of Egypt or Greece, or of the Native American tradition. There is no reason why he or she may not work with Merlin or Odin, or Quetzacoatl. These mythological or magico-religious systems are all levels of consciousness, laid one atop the other, though not one of them is in any way spiritually superior to the others. In personal terms, as an Englishman of Celtic background and tone, pledged to the Horned God, I have occasionally felt compelled to work with the Egyptian pantheons also—and there is not one drop of Egyptian blood within me.

The only question that American readers need ask themselves about the systems of other nations is, do they appeal? Do they strike any chords within the heart? And the fact is, that while neophytes may fool themselves into thinking that they are studying old mythology in order to awaken near-forgotten gods, it is really these same gods who are studying *them* in order to awaken their potentials.

Again, as an Englishman, I should only write about what I know best, and have experienced. So if I am to give any example of how we may apply the Tree of Life to some apparently unstructured systems, then the best example I can give is that of the Arthurian cultus.

Several important writers have dealt with this elsewhere, in different ways, notably Christine Hartley in her *Western Mystery Tradition*, and Gareth Knight in his *Secret Tradition in Arthurian Legend*. Both of them insist that the tales within the Arthurian Cycle contain fragments of occult lore of incredible age, and that Arthur, Morgan le Fay and the rest were hereditary initiatic titles rather than specific historical personages.

In many ways the Arthurian images offer the best of both worlds: Christians and Pagans alike can find whatever they need within that tradition. I know many Christian magicians who resonate to the energies of Merlin; and no member of Wicca could possibly wish for a better contact than Morgan le Fay. The actual central figure of Arthur Pendragon was hailed throughout England, Scotland and Wales, among the Celts and the Anglo-Saxons; he was venerated all over Western Europe also, as far afield as Italy and Germany. In a strange but very potent way his cultus also staked a very important claim before that gate to the Otherworld known as Hollywood.

It is a major topic, and clearly there is no space here to go into much detail—especially about some of the Celtic equivalents—but I hope to throw out enough to excite the reader into his own researches.

### Arthur and Tiphereth

Arthur is central to the whole scheme. Without him it falls apart. He is a solar figure par excellence. Consider the three Magical Images of Tiphereth (see Figure 7):

*Child:* Arthur was born of an illicit (and magically arranged) union between Uther Pendragon and Igraine. The babe Arthur was spirited away by Merlin to be raised in the Forest Sauvage. The tales of his coming into this world depict him as a true Wonderchild.

*Priest-King:* Arthur was always more than just another regent. He was credited with amazing deeds of a spiritual nature. His court was more than a court and something of a holy assembly instead. Christine Hartley opines that "Arthur" was in fact an initiatic title handed down through the ages.

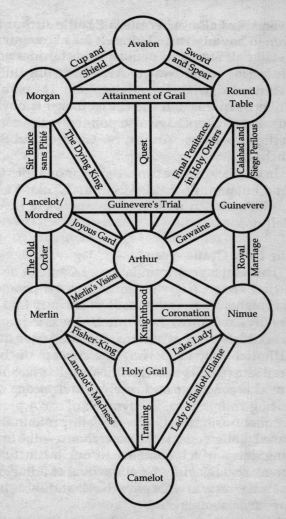

*Figure 7.*

*Sacrificed God:* After the last battle Arthur is seen to have sacrificed himself for his country. Yet like all Sacrificed or Solar Gods he does not die but is carried away to Avalon, resting until he is needed, when he will rise again. The parallel between this and the Christ image is obvious. Researchers have also pointed to the connections between Arthur, St. George, and St. Michael.

In Celtic terms we can see similar qualities in Cu Chulainn, Eochaid Airem and Tuan Mac Cairill; and also with Taliesin and Llew Llaw Gyffes.

## The Holy Grail—Yesod

This is the very foundation of Camelot and Arthur's reign. It is what transforms Arthur and his knights from a mere body of chivalry into a Goodly Company whose questing was in more than purely physical realms. The Grail gave the Arthurian epic its power. The concept of the Grail as a cup fits in well with Yesod's symbolism as a container and receiver and means of storing impressions. The symbols of cup, water, unconscious, and Grail are all profoundly linked. Thus Yesod is the powerhouse—the unconscious—which contains all our instinctual drives; and the Holy Grail's arrival at Camelot on Pentecost was what gave the Round Table its impetus, its *raison d'etre*.

The cauldron myths are close equivalents in

the Celtic realms of course, and notable examples are in those cauldrons or pots owned by Keridwen, Dagda, Bran, Matholwych and Pryderi.

## Camelot and Malkuth

This is the Western ideal of the perfect world, a gleaming, pleasant and secure place. Not heaven as such but an earthly equivalent, an accurate model. It is the sense of what we aspire to build in our own lives. The Irish parallel of the Four Holy Cities (Finias, Falias, Gorias and Murias) with the four Treasures (or Magical Weapons) forms a neat attribution to this Sphere too.

## Merlin and Hod

An obvious equation given Hod's link with the Hermetic Path. Merlin and Hod are both "initiators" in the sense that they begin things. It was Merlin's magic which enabled Uther to sleep with Igraine in the first place, while he is linked with both the Sword in the Stone and Excalibur. He was the guide and mentor of Arthur, a role which typifies Mercury's nature. He is omnipresent throughout the West though often with other names, such as Lailoken in the Celtic lands and Scottish borders. He is closely linked to the smith-gods which are so important in all European myths, so we can see parallels with Creidne, Govannon, as well as with more magical types such as Gwydion, Dian-cecht, Manawyddan and Mongan too, although that figure is more appropriate to the path connecting Hod and Tiphereth.

### Netzach and Nimue

Nimue or Vivienne, the young enchantress, the otherworldly creature of irresistible charm, a true Venus-figure. Merlin could not resist her, and no man can. She is seen as Fand, Doon Buidhe, Blodeuwedd (the "flower lady") and in negative aspect as the young Irish goddess Flidias, with her insatiable lust.

### Guinevere and Chesed

This is the sphere of stability and expansion and increase; the task of every king being to find himself a queen and ensure this. Without one the monarchy would be incomplete. In the earlier French versions Guinevere was far from being the silly feckless woman who ruined Camelot, but a force in her own right—learned, witty, humane, and popular. A fine equivalent is the goddess Bridget, or Bride, the hearth-goddess, while comparable figures include Etain, Grainne, and Olwen.

### Lancelot/Mordred and Geburah

Both of them in different ways managed to bring about Camelot's destruction, Mordred by design and Lancelot by the result of his love for the queen. They are alter egos to some extent. In some versions, however, it is Mordred who is Guinevere's lover and whose dark figure hearkens back to the Irish Mider, and earlier still to the Greek myths of the Underworld. Other figures include Diarmaid and Kulhwch.

## Morgan le Fay and Binah

Here we come to the Triple Goddess symbolism of the third Sphere, common to most mythologies. In this case we have the three sisters Morgana, Morgause, and Elaine. Sources differ as to which of the two former slept with Arthur, their half-brother, but for our present purposes Morgana is the better choice. She is the Queen Witch and her name means "sea-born"—reference to the "Bitter Sea" which is one of the esoteric titles of Binah. Thus in giving birth to Mordred, from her womb came the forces which eventually brought the breakdown of the cycle. She is directly equated with the Irish Morrigane, and her two sisters Babd and Macha, while Keridwen also is a major figure for Binah, as with Don and Danu.

## The Round Table and Chockmah

A single figure at this point could fit conveniently (such as Galahad and Perceval, both Grail-winners) but better still is the astrological image of the circle of the zodiac itself, which is the traditional "mundane chakra" for Chockmah. Not a single planet, understand, but the complete wheel of collective experience which totals Wisdom. The obvious parallel is that of the Round Table, a body of perfect men directed to the highest aspirations and balanced around a single point in harmony and equality. In Ireland we might consider, collectively, the gods of light known as the Tuatha de Danann, or Finn MacCumhail's "Red Branch Knights"; or else individual figures such as Dagda (connected with Morrigane), Lugh, the High God, or even Cu Chulainn again because of his peculiar dynamic nature, and whose whole death fastened to a single standing stone reeks of Chockmah symbolism at a certain level.

## Avalon and Kether

This is the heaven-point, where Camelot transcends toward the concept of the Holy Realm of Logres and its blissful otherworld of Avalon. Equivalents are to be seen in Annwn, and also in Tir na'n Og. However we must remember that Kether, however we analogize it, is always the highest concept to which we can possibly aspire. Avalon represents one possible attribution, but perhaps the best one is still that of God himself.

These are meant as guidelines only, for it is obvious that in the Celtic areas particularly, each image is open to much dispute. One advantage of these is that we have an immediate sympathy with them. We can use them just as well as the traditional correspondences as long as we can think of them as more than human figures. Whatever the demerits of the old archangelic images they at least have the advantage of being, for most of us, blank and clear forms without any suggestions of taint. We must therefore try not to think of Arthur as just some dirty but tough old Romano-British warrior who lived in the sixth century, but a veritable Sun-god of native traditions. Let us, then, look at a very simple rite which might help us get them fixed in such an attitude.

## Invocation

After all the preliminary work has been done, the magician faces east. Instead of Raphael however, this time he visualizes Merlin, according to his own conception of that Mage. He says: "Before me Merlin ... " The figure in this case is not wielding the sword but offering it to the magician. He remembers how Merlin is connected with the magical swords in the Arthurian cycle, and feels the breeze flowing against, indeed cutting through him. He feels the qualities of life, vitality, sharp intellect, and zestful questioning.

Turning to the south he acknowledges Arthur in the same way, instead of the sun-god Michael. He sees him with his spear or lance (called in Wales "Ron") and feels the qualities of light, strength, courage, authority and intuition flowing into waves of heat.

The west next, and the beautiful young Nimue. He sees her as through a pool. She carries the bejeweled and wondrous scabbard which had such potent healing powers, and the magician feels a sense of depth and tides, ebb and flow, and the qualities of love, passion, delight and rapture.

The north now and Morgana in starlight, holding the shield which was given to Galahad, emblazoned with a cross of ever-fresh blood, and the sense of slow growth and seasons, crops and plants around her, expressing the qualities of learning (in the experiential rather than the academic sense), endurance, maturity, tolerance.

Facing back to the east again he visualizes these figures around him then actually begins to walk slowly around the circle, clockwise, at each Quarter pausing to assume the role of that god-form and attempting to project the appropriate qualities. He circles inward, spiraling slowly to the center.

At the end of the rite, facing east once more, he turns to each Quarter and takes a slow breath, as he does so visualizing himself as absorbing each god-image, willing each one to take root within himself—willing himself to become a more complete person through these.

Again, we can tune ourselves into each

sphere by some more simple contemplations, which can be adapted according to the sexes:

1. You know Avalon if you have ever felt any kind of "heavenly homesickness" and an urge to return to the Source.

2. You understand the Round Table if you have ever felt uplifted by membership of a close and harmonious group or family.

3. You have felt Morgan if you have ever known the dark and brooding powers of Woman.

4. You know Guinevere if you have ever turned a house into a home—or loved two people equally at the same time.

5. If you have ever been drawn to the edge of madness by living too much, then you know Lancelot—or if you've ever fought for love.

6. If you have held a family or a workplace or a classroom together, and often suffered for it, then you know Arthur.

7. If you can recall the delights of infatuation, or wept in movies, then Nimue is not too far away.

8. The moment you practice magic, however simple, you become Merlin.

9. If you have dreamed of something greater than yourself, which could transform you, thenyou've glimpsed the Holy Grail.

10. If you have ever had an ideal of a perfect place to live, then Camelot beckons.

Now these are hardly high-powered philosophical questions, and they relate to only very simple aspects of the spheres concerned, but they do serve to show how we can make myths relate to our own experience.

### Arthurian Tarot

Obviously there is as much scope for this as for the foregoing. We can all design our own Tarot, but it does not necessarily have to take on a visual form. We do not actually have to draw the images. Again the scheme given on the paths here is meant as no more than a device to whet the student's appetite. There is not the space to go into detail but we could begin, for example, by comparing the Waite card "The Emperor" with the tales of Galahad and the Siege Perilous; or "The Tower" with Lancelot's castle of Joyous Gard where he eloped with Guinevere (previously called, incidentally, Castle Dolorous); or "The Magician" with the lame Fisher-King; or "The Hanged Man" with Arthur's death and his transport in the barge to Avalon in company with the Three Queens.

So what the reader must do now is find out as

much as he can about whatever mythology most appeals to his nature. The more he learns, and the more he plays around with the images by means of such master-glyphs as the Tree of Life or circle-cross, the more energy becomes available for making his magic come alive.

At the same time he can adapt every aspect of his daily life to this purpose. The more he studies mythology, even of the simplest kind, the more he will become aware that his own life is not that far removed from the great impulses symbolized by the most ancient tales.

# 9
# Group Work and the Individual

When we hear about ritual magic for the first time we inevitably conjure up visions of robed men and women in a circle. In a ritual based upon the circle-cross design, for example, the "officers" of the Quarters try to project the appropriate qualities to create the psychic interplay and balance of the forces of life, within a miniature cosmos of their own. This is rather like a gyroscope which depends upon the perfect balance of all its parts to stay in a constant position in regard to all else. Indeed, the gyroscope even looks like an expanded version of the circle-cross, and in a group ritual involving four people, each representing one of the Quarters, the same cyclic balance can be achieved. Eventually, though, the ideal is that you become the center or axis of your own cosmos rather than the outer periphery.

As to how group work can be so efficacious ...

We all know the great joy that derives from occasional gatherings with our nearest and dearest. There is a peculiar and very definite group-mind created which can cause simultaneous impulses within the whole group. Despite the diversity of characters there is nevertheless a remarkable sense of unity, and we learn from this. Qualities from others tend to rub off on us. It tends to provide a sense of deep well-being.

In group-work the aim is to create just such a harmonious unit, but one whose effects are likely to be even more far-reaching as the aim is toward Inner levels of amity. The efficacy of ritual work in groups is not because there is more power as such, but more harmony—more Wholeness.

The simple rituals given in earlier chapters can easily be worked with others. Instead of one person visualizing the god-forms of the Quarters, they can be represented by actual people, each one in harmony with his Element. They would be likely to meet seasonally, and thus align themselves with the earth's own sweep around the sun, and all its changes therein. They will align themselves with the natural harmony of things at magical levels and find balance within a chaotic world. In the earliest stages a good beginning might be for companions to jointly practice the exercises of Tarot "path-working," the whole group taking a journey through "The Moon" with one person directing out loud and asking the others in turn what they can see. A definite unity of response can result from this. The operators can be simply sitting next to each other with eyes closed and holding hands. Very simple. Very effective.

The moment a person begins to do magical work, he or she sends out a signal on the inner planes. If the work is steady and determined and thus produces a strong signal, then it will soon be answered—often in the most surprising ways. In due course people of similar affinities will be drawn into the orbit of the magician in question. The possibility of forming a group will arise.

The important thing is not *what* techniques are being used, but in the fact that the magician is actually doing *something*, regularly and with determination. The inner contacts, which are the true sources of magical energy, are not concerned with how naive or downright silly a person's first attempts at magic are, but in whether they are doing anything at all, with dedication and some attempt at originality. Besides, the word "silly" originally meant "holy." So there is no room in magic for those who might sneer at the early rituals and exercises of others.

Even so, the fact remains that some souls do seem fated never to be allowed access to any group, through no fault of their own. That was the case with myself. By the time that membership of such became available to me, I was no longer interested, and quite happy to continue on my own, with all the difficulties and the many freedoms that this entails.

Each person does in fact "belong." No matter how isolated they may be in physical and geographical terms, apparently consigned (or condemned) to a lifetime of solitary magic, they are actually part of one corporate whole. They are members of an inner group (tribe, clan, call it what you will) which exists partly in this world and partly in the next. Therefore, not all of the members are incarnate. And the earthly ones do not need to be connected in spatial terms.

The members of my own small "clan," for example, have gathered over many years. They are scattered over the world. We have never met *en masse* and never shall. Some of them have no overt interest in magic at all. Yet I know that each one is *there*, somehow, and part of me, and always has been, and that our individual work and consciousness in some strange way always gels.

I say this simply to offer the consoling message: we are never alone. The only danger to the student of magic is if he jumps into it too soon via the numerous commercial cults that exist. There is no denying the appeal of these. I personally wasted endless time and money on them—although even that was a test of my powers of discernment and discrimination.

There can be few Lamas, Galactic Magi and Great Masters who do not have my name on their mailing lists from years ago. The *real* magical groups are formed by those people who have gravitated toward each other and feel sufficient empathy to wish to share on deeper levels. As indicated, it is no more than a matter of very good friends who may or may not have shared previous lives together, and who may or may not have some spiritual potency, gathering together as would anyone else. To put the commercial groups into context, let us assume the reader has a group of people whose company he particularly enjoys, such as old school friends; or it might be a single person like a best friend or spouse. The companionship here is of paramount value in his life. He would not dream, therefore, of advertising in a magazine for other people to share this deep harmony, much less offer to teach it for a monthly fee.

Too often we are swayed by the claims of the self-styled Adepts. Claims which are made with incredible sincerity. In each case we hear ourselves asking: "He sounds like he means it. Why should he lie? He *must* be speaking the truth. Why should he lie?"

For power, adulation, wealth, an enraptured following, wealth . . . In this material world the question ought to be: Why *shouldn't* he?

Before they get smug, occultists are the most innocent of people in this respect. People do lie, of course they do. Or else they take drugs, or fool themselves. What often seems to occur is that the budding Great Master has a visionary experience of some sort. What he does, however, is credit the vision with intrinsic and external reality, and thus he becomes taken in by something which is only symbolic of unconscious elements within his psyche, having a quasi-validity at very best. Visions occur in Yesod, remember, the Moon and Sphere of Illusion. The crude levels of which are broached by psychedelic drugs or a raw natural psychism. This may well be why some of these cult figures are so very sincere about the most absurd teachings, because they really have seen *something*. On top of that, with a following of excitable and credulous people, the group-mind is enough to give the cultist some of the powers which he does claim. I suspect that this is why the Golden Dawn in its wisdom had a technique known as the "Testing of the Spirits" which was designed to check such delusions. If the "adept" in question had gone on to analyze his visions as pure symbols he might have gone on to something very potent indeed, instead of trapping himself at a low level.

In looking at all these cults we might take one great exemplar of Western spirituality—the figure of Christ—and ask ourselves: Would He teach by correspondence course? Would God reject us if we failed our monthly payments?

Would Jesus advertise in *Popular Mechanics*?

No, if we are sincerely committed to the magical and mystical path the right people will find their ways to us in good time. While all the occult powers that cults and sensational literature promise are far less important than the question of whether the magician is, at heart, a good and kindly person.

It will be seen, then, that there are countless levels of magical practice and training. We might draw a brief chart of these on Inner and Outer levels (see the following page).

A very simple and off-the-cuff chart to show the different approaches to magic in the lower Spheres, but one which is meant to imply that the outer levels are as sacred and capable of giving as much illumination as the inner.

In fact one of the so-called "Oaths" that used to be taken at a certain grade in the hierarchical structures of old systems was that we must come to view every event, action and circumstance as a direct and secret dealing between the spirit of the seeker and God. There is no reason at all why we cannot begin with this approach right away. Its value is that we come to see our outward circumstances in a very different light than before. And if we can direct our lives according to the highest qualities of the Tree, then so much the better.

Which is easier said than done, God knows.

|          | *Inner*                                                                              | *Outer*                                                                  |
| -------- | ------------------------------------------------------------------------------------ | ----------------------------------------------------------------------- |
| **Malkuth** | Magic Circles, Invocations, Creation of "Weapons" & Ritual Practices                 | Everyday World, Home, Work, Employment, Discrimination                   |
| **Yesod**   | Astral Magic, Evocation of Images, "Far Memories," Conditioning, Consciousness       | Dreams, Sex, Memories, Self-Awareness, Independence                      |
| **Hod**     | Occult Study, Analysis, Research into Magical Techniques, Meditation                  | Conversation, Travel, Communication, Reading, Observing, Musing          |
| **Netzach** | Magical Identification, Passionate Commitment, Occult Enthusiasm, Summoning of Energies | Romance, High Spirits, Rapture, Courtship, Pleasure                      |

There is no doubt that that much over-used word "karma" plays the major part in how or when—or even where—an individual makes links with like-minded souls. A person could feel inflicted by endless runs of bad luck, difficult circumstances which are not (apparently) of his own making, and ground down by unpleasant and recurrent situations at home or work.

All that anyone can ask for in these times is justice, pure and simple. Which is why the Egyptian god Thoth, Lord of Justice, was often regarded as *the* most important deity, for we can bear any hardship, any loss, if we can find a reason for it, or if we can believe that we are somehow paying our debts by suffering thus, or—best of all—if we surely know that matters will be redressed in our favor before very long. If justice is being done, or will be done on our behalf, then we can endure all things if we can believe this.

In grave situations within your own life, then, you can call up your own Lord of Justice. Whether this is Thoth in typical Egyptian form, or an aspect of the Christ, or the Dark Goddess even, does not matter so much as that your plea is a passionate and heart-felt one. You can do this in connection with any of the foregoing rituals and techniques. The plea itself should go something like this:

*If it is right and proper that I am being to made suffer this situation, or that Such-and-such is doing this to me, then I will try and accept it, and try to learn whatever lessons are necessary. Help me in this. But if this situation is unjust, and if Such-and-such is being completely unfair, then please redress the balance. Bring justice into my life.*

Create your own words along these lines, in your own speech rhythms. Imagine that you are offering your problem up to the deity in question.

And then sit back and wait.

The one thing you must realize is that if you are truly being made to learn some much-needed lesson in life, and if the problems *are* of your own making and no one else's, then this apparently simple magical act will bring the rest of the karmic energies through *at once*. If you were unhappy before, and cursed with seeming bad luck, then you will be staggered by what is about to come.

But at least the situation will be brought to a head very quickly, and you can get that karmic lesson over with more quickly than otherwise. And you *will* have a balance in your life at the end of it.

On the other hand, you may very well find that chronic problems clear up quite suddenly, that the hated Such-and-such is given his or her comeuppance in the most appropriate way. No true magician would ever actively curse another, because he who curses always has to pay a price for such an act, one way or another. But there is no reason why we should not call down the powers of Geburah in this manner and seek that level of Justice which is everyone's right.

# 10
# The Mysteries of Knowing

In the early chapter on the Tree of Life we briefly mentioned and then dismissed the sphere of Daath. We can look at this in a little more detail now because it gives us a glimpse of where humanity can go from here.

Daath means simply "knowledge." It is not knowledge in the intellectual, academic sense; it has nothing to do with university degrees or the ability to wrap up a simple concept in swathes of verbiage in order to give it a spurious substance. Daath is pure *experience*—or rather the impact that such experience has upon the psyche. When a man and a woman *know* each other in the old Biblical sense, then they are in touch with Daath.

Clearly Malkuth and Daath must be connected. The artist and occultist Austin Osman Spare touched on this in a crude, dark sort of way when he stated that "Knowledge is the excrement of experience." But then again he was a crude and dark sort of man. For polite purposes (not always the best or most effective) he might have said "Knowledge is the residue of experience." Or in yet other terms: Daath is the essence of Malkuth.

As the old Qabalists were quite concerned to point out, Daath was not a sphere as such. "The spheres number ten and not nine; ten and not eleven" they affirmed, because Daath was seen more as a potential, or a sense of immanence. Its traditional symbol is the Empty Room, which was the true secret of what actually lay behind the temple veil of the Holy of Holies. Daath was also the bridge across the dreaded Abyss which is so beloved of occult fiction writers.

It was the mystic and philosopher G.I. Gurdjieff who based his own spiritual system upon the notion that man has no soul, only a potential. This potential, he insisted, could be achieved only through inner work. And so at one level it was the Mysteries of Daath he was touching upon.

This may become clearer when we consider the esoteric belief that Malkuth's original position upon the Tree of Life was in fact at Daath. Thus the Tree, before the Fall, would have looked like Figure 8. This points to the belief that Mankind once existed as free and blissful spirits in a perfectly harmonious universe. The disharmony was caused when these free spirits "fell into matter." Fell into Malkuth. Prior to

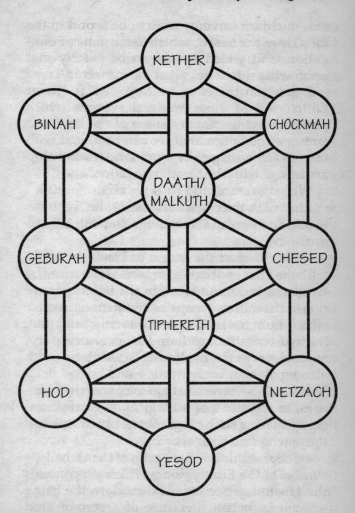

*Figure 8. The Perfected Tree*

that the lowest realms were to be found in the astral levels of Yesod, which name means Foundation, and which is seen to be exactly that upon what might be called the Perfected Tree.

Daath can therefore be regarded as "Inner Earth." All of those spiritual systems which posit the living consciousness of the land and embrace the notion that we can be united with the land in a magically symbiotic relationship are linked with the Daath revelation.

We experience, and thus we *know*.

Link with the consciousness of the Earth beneath, and we can *know* things that will help us touch the stars.

In this respect the magic of Daath is linked with the images of caves (or sometimes tunnels) within sacred mountains. In the latter case we find outstanding lumps of the densest matter which humans look to for heavenly salvation. Such mountains are found in every country, among every race. In almost all cases local myth also links them with mystic caves buried deep within. These caves are held to contain hero figures, or treasures of a magical, talismanic nature. Entering such caves invariably transforms those who find their way in.

Of course this is a clear echo of the Qabalistic symbol of the Empty Room which yet conceals the greatest of secrets. And modern life being what it is, occult literature of a certain kind abounds with tales of mysterious caves in mystic mountains which contain artifacts of stellar origin—advanced technologies from the most distant past. Writers such as Bulwer-Lytton, George Hunt Williamson, Erich von Daniken and Lobsang Rampa (to name just a few) have all touched upon this theme in different ways, although in truth we should not take any of them too seriously.

In this respect there is a hill near me which is said to be the home of Puck, the King of the Fairies. It was linked with the Knights Templar in medieval times. It is said to be hollow and contain the golden figure of a sacred ram. All of these things and more were said before the Space Age began. Now it is seen as the focus of massive UFO activity and is believed by some to contain a homing beacon for these craft, which some observers insist come from *within* the hill.

All of the latter are myths for our time, as C.G. Jung observed. In previous centuries men and women were "carried off" by fairies or demons. Now they are abducted by extra-terrestrials. All part of the Mysteries of Death if we but knew it.

Long before the present penchant for alien abductions (and let it be said now that hypnotic regressions "proving" the latter are probably the most inaccurate, deceptive, and largely useless techniques in the spiritual repertoire)—long before these became popular, magicians were making active use of the "Cave in the Mountain" imagery. My book *Twentieth Century Magic* contains the diaries of Charles Seymour from the late 1930s, in which this genuine Adept describes his contact with the inner-plane entity known as Cheiron, an otherworld being who helped him write "The Old Religion." As an essay on self-initiation into the Pagan mysteries of what was termed the "Green Ray," this has yet to be surpassed. According to Seymour this entity Cheiron had (and has) an evolutionary interest in humanity, and was linked—obviously—with the star-system of Alpha Centauri. Obviously because Cheiron was, in mythological terms, the leader of all the centaurs according to Greek tales. The information and energies that Seymour channeled from Cheiron was of a very high order indeed, but more important for our present purposes contains all the themes of Man and Nature linking with the stars by means of an empty space within a holy mountain.

When Seymour visualized that cave within his imagination, and in a very real sense entered therein to meet Cheiron, he *knew* that this was a genuine experience in another dimension. But the important thing is that none of us needs to accept this on trust. We must find our *own* knowing, our own gnosis. We must experience the world of matter in our own way, as already stated, and draw energies into that Empty

Room or Mystic Cave which lies within our own psyches.

We can make a beginning by using any of the ritual or imaginative techniques already described to prepare clear conditions for a Working. If you already know of a sacred mountain, or site of any kind which appeals to you (and don't worry about anyone else) then either go there—literally—or build it up in your imagination as intensely as possible. If you are actually there then make simple acknowledgments to the resident spirits, and then to the Elements, before visualizing a cave buried deep within the earth. Visualize yourself stepping out of your body and making your way through the ground toward it. If you are unable to be there in the flesh then visualize a narrow road leading to the place in question, rising gradually to a mid-point on the mountain slopes. Visualize a narrow fissure where your rocky path ends. Step through this and on and down a long, subterranean passageway which gleams with its own light. Try to sense the massive weight of the rock and minerals around you, increasing as you descend. At the end of the passage see a heavy and impossibly ancient door, bearing the symbol of the equi-armed circle-cross which is the oldest (and safest) of all images, and notice the brilliant shafts of light which spear out from the gaps between the door and its frame. Pause, take a breath, and open that door . . .

Figure 9.

This and many variations of the same has become almost a standard technique for making a direct link with what some might call Guides, others Guardians, and others still "inner contacts." It is impossible to say what you will see. It may be no more than a radiance with a very strong sense of presence behind it, which may or may not make its identity clear with further contacts. It may be something visually startling, such as a clear and very real image of whatever entity looks after the seeker's best interests. Or—it must be faced—nothing very much may *seem* to happen at all. But even in the latter case the magician is still expanding his consciousness and experience by his very effort, and this will come to have effects that will only gradually be apparent. The Empty Room within the psyche will start to sparkle. Gnosis will begin.

The foregoing technique can be bolstered if the magician can procure or bring back an actual piece of rock from the sacred place in question. After that, no matter where he might be in geographical terms, he can always put himself "in touch" with his power-source—quite literally—holding the stone while working at the purely visual techniques described.

Failing that, crystal is a wondrous aid. The magician can mentally project the image of the sacred mountain into the crystal and carry on the Working as given. Failing *that*, he or she can use a smoke-blackened mirror, or a bowl of dark liquid, or any of the traditional scrying aids to effect entry into this Cave.

It is while we do Work of this nature that we sometimes touch upon the highest aspects of talismanic magic—although these can often distract us from the true nature of Daath, and cause the Empty Room to become very cluttered indeed. It is the knowledge that matter is, or can be, imbued with spiritual energy. That lumps of crystal, for example, can help to transform us from within. In another area the practice of alchemy sought to transmute base matter into gold and bring the alchemist to immortality along the way. And although modern scientific knowledge discourages most people from practicing this art today, there is no reason why they could not, for example, create a system based upon home wine-making! The stages of fermentation can be made to parallel the traditional alchemical stages exactly; the act of gathering the raw material from a particular holy site at a particular time can be made into a Wiccan-type act in its own right. And at the end of it the alchemist *will* actually have something which can (legally) alter consciousness for sacerdotal purposes. When I did it myself using dandelions from the foot of Glastonbury Tor, my purpose was not to achieve the Philosopher's Stone, so much as to become Philosopher Stoned, in the most genteel of senses.

In truth the wine I made was dreadful. But

the experience of making it was something else.

The Mysteries of Daath are perhaps more closely entwined with the concept of Time than those of any other sphere. As Henri Bergson wrote "Time is the ratio of the resistance of Matter to Spirit." When the two are united we become outside of Time. In an area of consciousness where Time does not exist. A space between the worlds which parallels the cave within the Mountain.

There is one level in which we can regard this space as the gap between what we are, and what we *know* we should be. It is the gap between what our mortal warps and quirks compel us to persist in being, and that which our inner spark is quite certain we could be. Most of us spend a lifetime trying to cross that gap, or in despair because we do not know how, or else are afraid to try. All of this, on a purely psychological level, is but a lower analogue of that dreaded Abyss in which the evil and the nightmares of the entire universe can be found, and which Daath is said to straddle.

So at the simplest level the Mysteries of Daath teach us how to cross the gap between where we are, spiritually, and where we will to be, by the act of knowing ourselves. By holding firm to whatever self-gnosis we achieve, we can pluck up the courage to traverse our own nightmares. We can get closer to the Source.

This gap, this Abyss, also has another function which Austin Spare hinted at in the earlier mentioned quote, and which W.G. Gray states quite explicitly in his *Ladder of Lights*, in which he shows the Abyss to find its physical parallel in humans within the eliminative system. That is, there is a psycho-spiritual function within us which is quite able to break down bad memories and personal trauma in such a way as they can be—in effect—excreted from our system. Used accordingly, such waste matter will find its own place, ultimately providing a fertilizer that can benefit everyone. Modern psychology, unable or unwilling to accept the necessity or possibility of such a function, is all too often guilty of reaching into cesspools.

This may sound grim, or disturbing, but the process of knowing yourself must necessarily take in some truly abysmal revelations. In the old tradition this gap/crack/abyss—call it what you will—could be traversed by walking over a Bridge of Swords, the latter themselves being known as the Swords of Truth. In brief, truth hurts. Self-truth most of all. We can get all cut up. And if we are not mercilessly honest with ourselves, if we are not fearless and extremely well balanced, then we can fall in and spend the rest of our life wallowing.

No, it really isn't easy. Which is why we need some help from those entities on the other side who have our evolutionary interests at heart.

# 11
# Egyptian Magic

When we begin to put all these themes and techniques together for the first time, and perhaps try to take steps away from the Judaeo-Christian emphasis of the traditional Qabalah, it is often easier to start off using the Egyptian system. Not that the techniques themselves bear any resemblance to that which would have been practiced during the Pyramid Age, for example, but because the energies involved present themselves via imagery which has become almost universalized over the millennia. Besides which the Egyptian deities had such specific forms that they are actually quite easy to visualize. In contrast, the spirit of Baldur, for example, may have vast appeal for the intending practitioner of the Norse tradition, but his actual appearance is a matter for individual whim. For the novice, attempts to assume such a god-form often result in a kind of visualized fuzziness and uncertainty which can detract from the rest of the exercise. But with Egyptian Magic, as it has been developed over the past century at least, the lines and colors and postures of the deities can be seen in countless sources, with only minor variations.

### The Ka Posture

We can begin our work with the *ka* posture. It involves no more than standing with feet together and arms raised as in Figure 10. Now done in such a spiritless fashion the *ka* posture is an empty little exercise. But we can fill it with great energy with surprising ease.

By simple and subtle alterations of the hands (i.e. by making them clenched or open, facing upward or forward, straight or tilted), we can make the *ka* posture express rage or victory, supplication or surrender. Sportsmen constantly and unconsciously express the *ka* posture when they have won their event, and are in the throes of exultation. With only the simplest changes the same gesture is used by soldiers surrendering. Someone who has had great and unexpected luck will often glance upward and fling his arms likewise in a *ka* posture of thanks to the deity responsible.

Try a variety of such postures, varying the angle and inclination of the arms and the body, adopting the appropriate mannerisms for each emotion. But at the same time try to feel the emotion concerned: triumph or delight, plead-

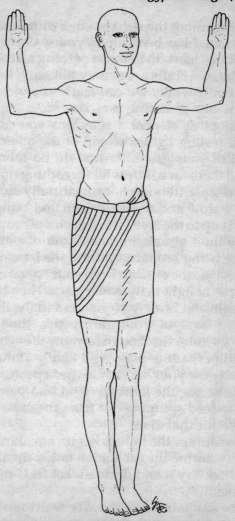

*Figure 10. The Ka Posture (illustration by Billie John).*

ing, yearning, or perhaps even divine submission to a greater Will than yours. Great actors and magicians do this sort of thing all the time, for the two crafts are closely linked.

After a while, we can learn to synchronize this with a breathing exercise.

Adopt as elegant a stance as you can, one hand resting lightly on top of the other at the level of your groin. At first do no more than stand there for a little while breathing regularly and deeply (though not unnaturally so). Then take a slow and deeper breath and bring your hands up to the level of your solar plexus, at the same time visualizing a column of pure brilliance being brought up from the base of your spine. Breathe out, but keep your hands and the column of light in the same place. Then breathe in again and bring your hands and the light up to the level of your throat this time, your thumbs linked as though forming the symbol of a bird in shadow-play. And finally at the third breath raise your hands into the *ka* posture itself while seeing the light carry on into your head and indeed spuming out from the crown during your exhalation.

Sometimes the light takes on a real inner intensity during the exhalation rather than the inhalation. Try it and decide what feels right for yourself.

The fountaining light can be seen to spray out into the shape of the auric egg as described in the Exercise of the Middle Pillar in an earlier chapter. And at this point similar work can be done in terms of color visualization and energy projection.

Once a degree of mastery has been achieved with this, we can also build into it exercises relating to the endocrine system. As detailed in *The Inner Guide to Egypt*, written by myself and B. Walker-John, the Ancient Egyptians truly believed that their country was an earthly mirror for the heavens above, and that Man was an expression of them both. That is to say certain Mystery Centers of Ancient Egypt could be seen as earthly analogues of certain stellar energies; while at the same time these earthly and stellar centers found direct equivalents within the endocrine glands of similar function.

Thus starting at the bottom, the testes or ovaries would equate with the energies of Thebes; the pancreas would relate to the Mysteries of Abydos; the adrenal glands linked with Hermopolis; the thymus with Memphis; the thyroid and parathyroid with Heliopolis; the pineal with Khebit; and lastly the pituitary with Alexandria.

The actual Egyptian names of these places can then be turned into "Words of Power" which are no less effective than the Hebrew god-names used in traditional Qabalistic exercises.

(For the sake of the present exercise, and for

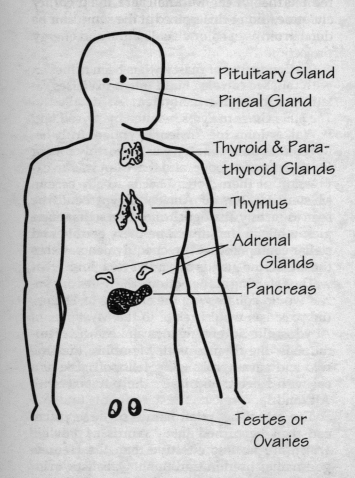

*Figure 11. The Endocrine Glands*

reasons that we cannot detail here, the pituitary and pineal can be energized at the same time as the thyroid.)

| Center | Egyptian Name |
|--------|---------------|
| Thebes | Uas (*Wass* or *Wast*) |
| Abydos | Abtu |
| Hermopolis | Khemnu |
| Memphis | Men-nefer |
| Heliopolis | Aunu |

Visualize these centers on your body as jewels which glow accordingly when the rising light touches them. Synchronize your breathing as you see fit. You need not worry about exact pronunciations of each word, or exact patterns of inhalation. Just work at it, and find what works best for you.

### Astral Masks

Again, in time, a new phase can be introduced in this exercise of the *ka* posture, and one which involves the donning of astral masks as a preliminary to assuming the full god-form.

What the magician must do first is find any book which may contain details of the Egyptian gods and goddesses. Read as much as possible about their functions. Horus, for example, can be seen in simple terms as the young warrior god, champion of light, destroyer of darkness. Assuming the appropriate *ka* posture for these

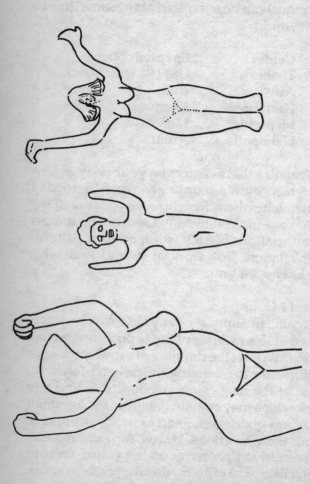

Figure 12. Archaic figurines in the ka position c. 4000–3500 BC. The larger female figure on the left is the prehistoric image of the Goddess (illustration by Billie John).

*Figure 13. The ka statue of King Auibre' Hor of the 13th Dynasty from his tomb at Dahsur (illustration by Billie John).*

qualities, then visualize also the Horus hawk-head upon yourself. Not just as a convenient addition to your own cranium, but an actual transformation of yourself. Do this while intoning the name Heru (the true version of Horus) in whatever manner is most resonant.

Men or women can do this exercise, although the latter may prefer the vulture-goddess of Mut, or the lion-goddess Sekhmet, who had great powers of healing as well as a willingness to tear apart anyone who might harm her children.

The same work can be done with Anubis, the jackal-god known as the Opener of the Way whose metabolism is able to derive spiritual energies from what others might see as dead meat; in other words, bright wisdom from the most dismal experience.

Osiris, the fertility god, is invariably human in form but he wears the splendid headpiece, the atef-crown, which proclaims him as Lord of the Underworld and also a Horned God. His true name is Asar.

All of the strange animal or bird heads, all of the headpieces, such as the vulture wings or crescent moon, all of these provide sharp and easily visualized symbols that we can build into our self-imagery as we use the *ka* posture.

We can also begin to ask ourselves the same series of questions that we described earlier:

Have you ever felt young and vigorous and a champion of truth and fair play? Then you can link with Horus.

Have you ever held down a good job and built up a home? Then you can know Isis— whose true name is Aset.

Have you ever made anything grow? (No need to be too literal here.) Then you can know Osiris.

Have you ever kept yourself to yourself and reveled in secrets? You can make links with Nephthys.

Have you ever experienced death and gained insights from it? You can make contact with Sokaris.

Have you ever gained personal power from confronting the dark aspects of your psyche? Then you can know Anubis.

Have you ever tried bringing order into a chaotic situation? Then you can link with Maat.

Have you ever enjoyed knowledge for the sake of knowledge? Then you can know Thoth.


And on and on and on, throughout the massed pantheons of a lost realm which still exists within us. A vital part of the magic is actually learning how to ask ourselves these questions.

If we wish to tie all of this in with the afore-
mentioned imagery of the Qabalah itself, perhaps by associating the Egyptian deities with
the Spheres, then there is infinite scope for the
individual.

One could, for example, decide to work with
the Sphere of the Moon, known in the Qabalah
as Yesod, but which would in the Egyptian
scheme fit in quite nicely with Thebes, and the
Moon-gods there, as well as with the ovaries,
the Mysteries of Women, and the months of the
year. Using the Tarot card The Moon as a gate-
way you could visualize yourself going between the two towers and across the brow of the
hill into the Temple of Mut, the great vulture-
goddess whose name is actually a root for
"mother," and whose temple was once fronted
by a sacred lake shaped like the embryo in the
womb. No need to give here one of those "path-
workings" which are so often merely an excuse
for the writer to indulge to purple prose. If Mut
wants you, if she has any resonance at all within
your psyche, she will be more than happy to
help you create a very real path of your own toward her.

The main thing to bear in mind, always, is
that it is just as unwise to mix magical systems
as it is to mix drinks. If you decide to fashion
something along Egyptian lines, it should not
involve archangels from the particular Sphere

Isis

Horus

Ptah

Sekhmet

Ra

Thoth

(illustrations on pages 157–159 by Billie John)

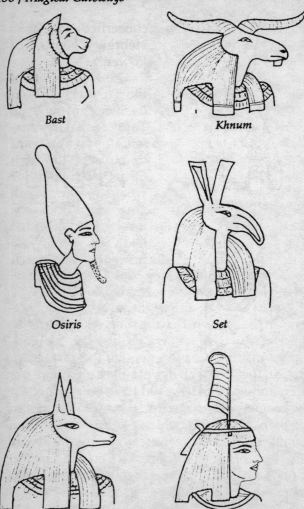

Bast

Khnum

Osiris

Set

Anubis

Maat

*Amun*

concerned, or use Hebrew "Names of Power."

The framework of the Tree of Life is in itself neutral (as is the Tarot to a large extent), but if you want to build it up with Egyptian imagery or whatever, then when you begin to work through it you must learn to switch off from the traditional version before switching onto whatever frequencies you have now decided to use.

Which is why, although the Egyptian "centers" in the *ka* posture have direct parallels with the Hebrew Sephira, we do not use the god-names of the latter to energize the former. In fact, if the original Egyptian names had not been known then it would have been better for the magician to make up "nonsense" sonics of his own. Just as ridiculous nicknames between lovers can take on real meaning and influence between the people concerned, so can fanciful sounds be used for the highest magical purposes.

# 12
# Past Lives Revisited

One of the things which invariably happens
when a person begins and sustains magical
work, is that circumstances arise, dreams or visions develop, which seem to indicate the certainty of a past life.

Of course, one of the immediate criticisms
provoked by all those antagonistic to the whole
magical process is that such experiences are no
more than compensatory boosts to the ego.
Without having the slightest experience of such
things themselves, or of any intimacy with
genuine practitioners of the art, they invariably
invoke names like Cleopatra or Napoleon to
poke fun and give themselves an air of de-
tached wisdom. While there certainly are inadequate individuals who do seek to gain substance by claiming to have been someone exalted from history, these same individuals
could never undergo real magical training.
They would make these claims however their

lives progressed. In practice, however, none of the genuine Adepts of my acquaintance have ever shown any great interest in who they may have been in earlier epochs. They were (and are) too busy getting on with their Work in this life to be hooked on past lives. Only Christine Hartley, whose far memories are adequately recorded in my *Twentieth Century Magic* gave a reasonably exalted identity as Merit-aten, a princess from Ancient Egypt. But it was a matter of supreme indifference to her whether anyone else believed her, and her everyday life was extraordinary enough as it was, without taking into account her magic. And as she herself said, princesses in Ancient Egypt were a dime a dozen. It was no great deal.

Even so, the topic of reincarnation is by no means as simple as the standard philosophy would seem to suggest. There is no doubt that "far memories" gained from hypnotic regression are always immensely detailed, and emotionally convincing, but tests have shown again and again how inaccurate those details really are. That is not to say that *all* hypnotic regressions are no more than visionary deceptions, but they are best admired as demonstrations of the mind's wonderful ability to create cohesive epics that are essentially fictional in nature. Which does not mean that we cannot get wisdom and delight from such things. But no one should accept that a thing has been "proved" because it was demonstrated by the process of hypnotic regression.

Quite often, also, a person can tune in to past events in the most unexpected circumstances. Such events can replay themselves before his inner vision with immense lucidity. This is the idea that certain places can retain their own memories, stored away within the stones like on a videotape, and spontaneously replaying themselves to the astonished inner gaze of particular souls. The latter may experience these so intensely that the assumption is made of having gone through these events in a past life. It may well be so, but there is also the possibility to consider that he was acting as no more than a receiving apparatus.

Yet another possibility which can affect the whole experience of "far memory" is the fact that when a magician makes contact with an inner-plane entity of historical fact, images and experiences of the entity will often filter through into the magician's consciousness. Often, he can be tempted to think he *was* that entity in question. It is a natural temptation. Everyone succumbs to it for a little while in the early phases of magical work.

All of which can go toward explaining why the gods are supposed to destroy whoever becomes guilty of hubris—or overwhelming pride.

It is never because the gods feel challenged,

and thus determined to humble the wretch concerned. It is because hubris stops the magician from becoming a clear and effective channel for their energies. The magician can no longer do the Work as it should be done. So the gods withdraw and leave him to deal with their echoes and shells only; and soon the man destroys himself.

When the magician first plugs into what might be termed a "Magical Current"—which, like Time, is experienced but almost impossible to define—external events occur which seem to be clear examples of some cosmic power sending "signs" to confirm the veracity of the contact. These events often take the form of reincarnational sagas involving groups of people.

For example, in the early 70s I began work on an as yet unpublished novel based around the isle of Lindisfarne in the 7th century. Lindisfarne is an island only a mile off the northeast coast of England, reachable twice a day by road when the tide recedes, and regarded by many as one of the major power-centers of Britain. Historically it ranks alongside Iona as one of the last bastions of Celtic Christianity, was the source of the dazzling and illuminated Lindisfarne Gospels, and was seen to keep the light of Civilization flickering at a time when it was going out all over Europe. No sooner had I started writing than people began to appear in the most unlikely and unexpected ways, all of whom had Lindisfarne fascinations for the same period. The name itself would crop up in every conceivable source: in newspapers, magazines, on television documentaries, or on the radio via the songs of the once-famous folk-rock group of that name. Always appearing at apparently crucial or significant moments, though often in the most insignificant ways, and always with a staggering frequency of occurrence.

On and on this went, a saga involving incredible levels of coincidence, drawing in many people who became as surprised as myself, the events and their omens circling around my own life constantly, but never *quite* linking up in any solid mandala of revelation.

My conclusion at that time was that I had once been a monk on Lindisfarne—perhaps even the Prior—and that the rest of the events could be explained by the concept of group reincarnation. Really it was a delicious time. For a number of years I lived with the notion that once, in the Dark Ages, I had been a monk on a tiny island amid the gray sea with seals and gulls for company.

However, I eventually had to admit the historical details which presented themselves in a variety of ways were wrong. Sure, they possessed enough half-truth and quasi-possibility to lead me down many false paths, but at the end of the day there was no avoiding the fact that they were wrong. End of story.

As far as I can explain it now (and explanations are not always wise or necessary) the act of brooding upon Lindisfarne acted like the touch upon the keyboard of some cosmic computer. The computer itself, which exists in all dimensions, did no more than display before me all the references it had on that topic, doing so in a multitude of experiential ways even though the references (like identical names in a telephone directory) did not necessarily bear any relationship to each other.

Not so much egg on the face as ego on the face, but every magician goes through this sort of thing. It is enthralling while it lasts. The only danger lies in getting hooked on the twists and turns of the apparent saga, rather than concentrating on the energy behind it.

Yet over and above all of these "explanations" for what seems to be reincarnation, many people still do have experiences in which they know to their bones that they have lived before in a particular place at a particular time. This knowledge can be so intense, so impossible to articulate, that the person concerned has no compulsion to tell anyone else, no burning desire to seek documentary proof. Knowing with all your heart can be enough.

Personally I believe that while reincarnation of the "classical" kind does occur, it is by no means universal. We are not all guaranteed a return. I believe that it does happen in the case of sudden or violent death. Or else when the magician or mystic concerned is so closely attuned in his own lifetime to his own Higher Self.

As I have written elsewhere, quoting the words of Charles Seymour, a personality incarnates but never reincarnates. It is the Higher Self which does so, sending little bits of itself into incarnation each time in order to gain experience. Thus a particular Higher Self (regard it as a group mind/soul, or superconscious corporate entity) can have numerous souls in incarnation at any one time—even extending *through* time. It is perhaps not so much that we have previous lives, as *other* lives. Like the beads on a necklace, all connected by the same thread. Glimpses we may have of what seem to be previous lives can often be other aspects of our own Higher Self as they exist in a different time. Parts of ourselves, in fact. We are one another, all over again.

To this extent I believe that a part of myself once existed (or exists) in the 19th Dynasty of Ancient Egypt as a junior scribe. Also that this link helped Billie John and myself to bring through that relatively complete and "new" magical system described in our *Inner Guide to Egypt*. All of which was under the aegis of the entity shown in Figure 15.

But if all this could somehow be disproved tomorrow it would cause me no devastation at all. Life is too short for that.

Figure 15. (illustration by Billie John).

## Techniques for Recall

All of this said and done, it is human nature to try and stimulate what may or may not be genuine far memories of a genuine past life. Christine Hartley reached a stage toward the end of her life where she simply created a blank screen before her mind's eye and asked her inner contacts to show her what she wanted/needed to know.

The trick behind this at one level is to act like we do when we play games with very young children, watching them while pretending not to. It helps to concentrate on the breath as it goes in and out of our nostrils, visualizing it as pure light, while at the same time keeping the inner gaze lightly upon the blank screen. Pictures arise with surprising ease but these are quickly broken if the startled viewer turns his full consciousness onto them. Again, they are not necessarily from past lives. They may not be more than the astral equivalent of junk mail. Which is why a preliminary invocation to whatever entity the magician thinks appropriate should be used.

Many of the visualization techniques are akin to path-workings. We can add a simple piece of tactile back-up here by making our own Mobius Strip. This is made by taking a narrow length of paper and bringing the two ends together to form a loop. Just before you do so, however, give one of the ends a half twist and then join them up. If you study this loop you will find that it actually has become a figure with one side. Inside and outside has ceased to exist. A continuous pencil line can be drawn around it without having to take the point off the paper. The visualization techniques can be run through while the magician sits quietly running this through his fingers like a trans-dimensional rosary.

The fingers will be reminding the subconscious that ultimately there is no outer and no inner, no past and no future, and that they are all one. The imaginative faculty, meanwhile, can be working through whatever sequence of visualizations have been chosen, although at a certain point you should keep the fingers still upon the loop-over point and just hold the Mobius Strip.

The visualization itself could go something like this . . .

Picture yourself standing outside your body looking at yourself as you sit or lie in a relaxed, secure manner. Then imagine yourself shrinking into a tiny pinpoint of light—shrinking into your essence. As Aleister Crowley once said, "Every Man and Woman is a Star," and you might think of your essence as being like this, with your body vast before you.

Close up on your own face. See it filling your whole vision, the pores like craters. See the ajna chakra—the third eye—like a whirling, multicolored vortex. Feel the auric currents around your body rising and falling like the sea as you breathe in and out.

Then, with an act of will, move into the ajna's vortex, spinning around and down, into your own forehead and the velvet night of the brain cavity.

We all know what the brain actually looks like. Look up an illustration after reading this and fix upon the main parts. Picture it like an asteroid in the depths of interstellar space. A lump of living rock, lined and fissured. Circle it. Be aware of the two halves. Look at the cerebrum and cerebellum. It is in the latter, tucked away on the underside, that our minute and concentrated spark of consciousness must go. Float to the front of the cerebellum and see the great mass of the rest of the brain above. See one of the lines between the convolutions open out into a crack, and then a clear opening. Head into it, toward the heart of the cerebellum itself, twisting and turning through what seems like a maze. Here, in the middle of the most ancient part of the brain, find yourself in a crystalline cave, the walls of which you just know can reflect images from your own ancestral memories at least, and perhaps beyond these to something else again.

Ask whatever higher power you cleave to for permission to see what needs to be seen. And then wait ...

Whatever happens, whatever you experience, as always return by the same route and then write down whatever you remember, no matter how trivial this may seem.

Such techniques as the latter are more effective when done with the help of someone, preferably of the opposite sex, holding hands and having one partner narrating the journey and the other experiencing it. In reality not everyone is able to find such a willing partner, and their spouses, no matter how loving and supportive they might be in other areas, are not necessarily in sympathy with this aspect of their partners' natures.

Yet there is a simple and undemanding party trick by which anyone can demonstrate to themselves, and others, the ease with which visions can be made to arise. Once done, the intending magician can then approach his or her own path-workings with a new sense of confidence.

At any small, congenial gathering, where there are no major distractions, you can offer to demonstrate a five minute psycho-analysis to any willing volunteer. This can be done at a dinner table or sprawled around the living room—the more casual the circumstance the better. Insist upon the lighthearted nature of the experiment. Do not try to drag in occult overtones. Tell the rest of the party that they can participate also as long as they keep quiet, and wait until afterward to share their own experiences. Tell the volunteer that he need simply sit back and listen while you present to him the outline of an imaginary journey, marked by various stages, all of which can yield to psychological interpretations which you will describe later.

1. Tell the volunteer to imagine that he is in a wood. Ask him what sort of wood it is (i.e. dark and menacing, light and cheery, deciduous or evergreen, etc.). Ask him what season it is. What he can see as he looks around. Then ask him how he feels about being there in the wood. Is he happy? Intimidated? Anxious?

(What invariably happens is that the imagery builds up with such strength that you will not need to "lead" the person at all, just ask him questions so that you can get a good idea of what he is seeing.)

2. Tell him that there is a path stretching before him. Again, get him to describe the path.

3. As he now walks along this path tell him that he finds a key lying on the ground before him. Get him to pick this up and describe it, as before.

4. Further along he finds a cup. Question as before.

5. Further still he comes to a clearing in the middle of which is a massive bear—and an extremely menacing one. Tell him that he has to get to the other side somehow. Get him to describe how he will do this, in any way that he

wants.

6. He then comes to a body of water. Question as before. Ask him how he plans to get across it.

7. On the other side is a wall which he soon comes to. It stretches from one side of the world to the other, as far as the eye can see. Propped against it is a ladder. Get the volunteer to climb the ladder and describe what he sees on the other side.

End of party game.

Now insist at this point that the interpretations which you will give are for fun only (and they are), and most certainly not to be taken seriously.

Thus the wood will represent how the volunteer views his life at the moment—cheery or scary, dark or delightful, wintry or in full summer. The path through it a symbol of how he sees his own progress, whether this is via muddy twists and turns, getting nowhere, or on a broad dry path. The key is a symbol of the ego—small or massive, bright or dull. The cup, a symbol of the emotional state. How a person deals with the bear in the clearing is a symbol of how he tends to confront problems—head on, or sneaking around the side. The body of water is a symbol of the sex drive. The wall on the other side is a symbol of death, and of what a person might expect to see on the other side.

It cannot be emphasized too strongly here

that this is a lighthearted game, no more, best done among friends after a few glasses of wine. When the Welsh poet David Annwn did this to me many years ago (and this is always a one-off) my key was a massive device, bigger than a bazooka, which I could scarcely lift; my cup was a filthy cracked affair, disgusting inside; I hid from the bear and skirted around it; my body of water was a massive, seething lake, boiling with ichthyosaurii and other primitive creatures, which I crossed on the smallest of boats while giving Tarzan calls; but beyond the wall I saw ... marvelous things.

It is a laugh, no more (and what is wrong with that?); but after you've played this game a few times you can get a real sense of the possibilities behind true magical path-workings, such as you might find in *The Shining Paths* by Dolores Ashcroft-Nowicki, which is effectively an experiential exploration of the Tree of Life using its deepest symbolism. You can then go on with some confidence to fashion something for yourself that may or may not involve others. As will happen with such magic, the effectiveness of this party game develops as you think of the best ways to put it across to each person. No good reading from a script. No good being ponderous or pompous. Do it with friends, for the friendliest of purposes, and work your magic likewise.

The true disciplines of magic are never easy,

as I've said time and time again, but there is no reason why we should not have a little fun along the way. And if you can't occasionally learn to poke fun at yourself, then don't even bother making the journey inward.

# Conclusion

By now you will have within your grasp the essential techniques which form the backbone of the Western Magical Tradition as it has existed for most of this century and a little before. You can banish unpleasant atmospheres, purify places of working, build patterns in your aura and create gates into other dimensions. Your task now is to use these techniques and improve upon them, thus making sure that this same Tradition in a century's time has gone on at least a few steps. Never get bogged down by dogma, or timidity; set no limits on your imagination. Work your magic with all the passion, elegance, and basic human decency that you can command.

# Appendix

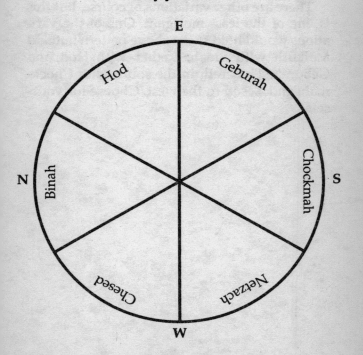

Figure 16.

This is just one interpretation of the Tree as arranged on the circle-cross. The Spheres of the Middle Pillar are held to form a central axis with Tiphereth at the center and, if we imagine that we are looking down upon a spherical shape, Kether at the top pole with Yesod at the bottom. Malkuth is the whole thing in itself.

There are other variations of course, but this is one of the least inelegant. One of the variations would hold to the above pattern but add Malkuth with Binah; Kether with Hod and Geburah; Tiphereth in the south with Chockmah; and Yesod to the west. Choose for yourself.

## Kether

| | |
|---|---|
| Mundane Chakra | ———— |
| Archangel | Metatron |
| God-Name | Eheieh |
| Magical Image | The face of a bearded patriarch shown in profile |
| Color | Brilliance |
| Symbols | The point within a circle, the node of the cosmic lemniscate, the crown |

## Chockmah

| | |
|---|---|
| Mundane Chakra | The zodiac |
| Archangel | Ratziel |
| God-Name | Jehovah, Yahweh, Yod He Vau Heh |
| Magical Image | A bearded male figure, full face |
| Color | Iridescent gray, flecked with light |
| Symbols | The straight line, the phallus, the rod |

## Binah

| | |
|---|---|
| Mundane Chakra | Saturn |
| Archangel | Tzaphkiel |
| God-Name | Jehovah Elohim |
| Magical Image | A mature woman |
| Color | Black, dark hues |
| Symbols | The cup, the lamp |

## Chesed

| | |
|---|---|
| Mundane Chakra | Jupiter |
| Archangel | Tsadkiel |
| God-Name | El |
| Magical Image | A benevolent king enthroned |
| Color | Blue |
| Symbol | The square, the cornucopia, laughter |

## Geburah

| | |
|---|---|
| Mundane Chakra | Mars |
| Archangel | Khamael |
| God-Name | Elohim Gibor |
| Magical Image | A stern king in his chariot |
| Color | Red |
| Symbols | The scourge, the sword, the pentagon |

## Tiphereth

| | |
|---|---|
| Mundane Chakra | The Sun |
| Archangel | Michael |
| God-Name | Jehovah Aloah va Daas |
| Magical Image | A child, a priest-king, a sacrificed god |
| Color | Salmon-pink, gold flecked |
| Symbols | The hexagram, the rose |

## Netzach

| | |
|---|---|
| Mundane Chakra | Venus |
| Archangel | Auriel |
| God-Name | JHVH Tzavoos |
| Magical Image | A beautiful, naked female |
| Color | Emerald |
| Symbols | The girdle, the seven-pointed star |

## Hod

| | |
|---|---|
| Mundane Chakra | Mercury |
| Archangel | Raphael |
| God-Name | Elohim Tzavoos |
| Magical Image | A hermaphrodite |
| Color | Orange-yellow |
| Symbols | The caduceus, the serpent |

## Yesod

| | |
|---|---|
| Mundane Chakra | The Moon |
| Archangel | Gabriel |
| God-Name | Shaddai el Chaiim |
| Magical Image | A powerful, naked man |
| Color | Violet-blue |
| Symbols | The cup, the mirror |

## Malkuth

| | |
|---|---|
| Mundane Chakra | Earth |
| Archangel | Sandalphon |
| God-Name | Adonai ha Aretz |
| Magical Image | A crowned queen (Nature) |
| Color | Citrine, olive, russet, black |
| Symbols | Sandals, the altar |

# Useful Books

Books often seem to have their own innate power to make themselves appear when we need them. They come looking for us, even if we are completely unaware of them. Even so, we can give a few suggestions for worthwhile further reading.

*The Mystical Qabalah* by Dion Fortune is still the best book ever written on that subject. "Dion Fortune" was the pen name of a woman who died in 1946, and whose importance as a writer, magician, and visionary is only now being recognized. Her two novels *The Sea Priestess* and *Moon Magic* are without compare, and teach more about real magic than most technical books can ever hope to achieve. Among many other books she also wrote that curious and often intensely beautiful book *Psychic Self-Defence*, which is more a magical autobiography than anything else, and which gives numerous practical methods of proven effectiveness.

Those people who would like to go further into the QBL itself should read W.G. Gray's *Ladder of Lights*, which looks at the Tree from a completely different angle, and which is appropriately subtitled *Kabbalah Renovata*. And David Godwin's excellent *Cabalistic Encyclopedia* provides a dictionary of Cabalism as understood and interpreted by the various Hermetic societies of the West.

Israel Regardie's *Foundations of Practical Magic* contains his long essay "The Art of True Healing" which gave the first exposition of the Middle Pillar Exercise. While *The Magician—His Training and Work* by W.E. Butler has an atmosphere all its own.

In the realms of ritual magic pure and simple, there is the immensely practical *Temple Magic* by W.G. Gray again, *Modern Magick* by Donald Michael Kraig, and the *Ritual Magic Workbook* by Dolores Ashcroft-Nowicki.

These are suggestions only. In truth, the books you will most need are probably already making their cunning ways toward you—if they haven't already done so.

## STAY IN TOUCH

On the following pages you will find listed, with their current prices, some of the books and tapes now available on related subjects. Your book dealer stocks most of these, and will stock new titles in the Llewellyn series as they become available.

To obtain a FREE COPY of our latest full catalog of new titles as they are released, just write to the address below. In each 80-page catalog sent out bimonthly, you will find articles, reviews, the latest information on New Age topics, a listing of news and events, and much more. It is an exciting and informative way to stay in touch with the New Age and the world. The first copy will be sent free of charge and you will continue receiving it as long as you are an active mail customer. You may subscribe to *The Llewellyn New Times* by sending a $7.00 donation in the U.S.A. and Canada ($20.00 overseas, first class mail). Order your copy today!

*The Llewellyn New Times*
**P.O. Box 64383-Dept. 681, St. Paul, MN 55164-0383**

## TO ORDER BOOKS AND PRODUCTS ON THE FOLLOWING PAGES

If your book dealer does not carry the titles and products described on the following pages, you may order them directly from Llewellyn by sending full price in U.S. funds, plus $3.00 for postage and handling for orders *under* $10.00; $4.00 for orders *over* $10.00. There are no postage and handling charges for orders over $50.00. Postage and handling rates are subject to change. UPS delivery: We ship UPS whenever possible. Delivery guaranteed. Provide your street address as UPS does not deliver to P.O. Boxes. UPS to Canada requires a $50.00 minimum order. Allow 4–6 weeks for delivery. Orders outside the U.S.A. and Canada: Airmail—add retail price of book; add $5.00 for each non-book item (tapes, etc.); add $1.00 per item for surface mail. You may use your major credit card to order these titles by calling 1-800-THE-MOON, M–F, 8:00–5:00, Central Time. Send orders to:

**LLEWELLYN PUBLICATIONS**
**P.O. Box 64383-Dept. 681**
**St. Paul, MN 55164-0383, U.S.A.**

Prices subject to change without notice.

## 20TH CENTURY MAGIC AND THE OLD RELIGION
**by Alan Richardson**

This magical record details the work of two senior magicians—Charles Seymour and Christine Hartley—within Dion Fortune's Society of the Inner Light during the years 1937 to 1939.

Using juxtaposed excerpts from Seymour and Hartley's magical diaries together with biographical prefaces containing unique insights into the background and nature of the Society, Alan Richardson paints a fascinating picture of Dion Fortune and her fellow adepts at the peak of their magical careers.

Originally published as *Dancers to the Gods*, now with a new introduction and the addition of Seymour's long essay, "The Old Religion," a manual of self-initiation, this new edition retains Dion Fortune's "lost" novels, the past-life identities of her Secret Chiefs, and much more.

0-87542-673-5, 288 pgs., 6 x 9, photos　　　　　　$12.95

## ANCIENT MAGICKS FOR A NEW AGE
**by Alan Richardson and Geoff Hughes**

With two sets of personal magickal diaries, this book details the work of magicians from two different eras. In it, you can learn what a particular magician is experiencing in this day and age, how to follow a similar path of your own, and discover correlations to the workings of traditional adepti from almost half a century ago.

The first set of diaries is from Christine Hartley and shows the magick performed within the Merlin Temple of the Stella Matutina, an offshoot of the Hermetic Order of the Golden Dawn, in the years 1940–42. The second set is from Geoff Hughes, and details his magickal work during 1984-86. Although he was not at that time a member of any formal group, the magick he practiced was under the same aegis as Hartley's. The third section of this book, written by Hughes, shows how you can become your own Priest or Priestess and make contact with Merlin.

0-87542-671-9, 320 pgs., 6 x 9, illustrated　　　　　$12.95

## EARTH GOD RISING
### by Alan Richardson

Today, in an age that is witnessing the return of the Goddess on all levels, the idea of one more male deity may appear to be a step backward. But along with looking toward the feminine powers as a cure for our personal and social ills, we must remember to invoke those forgotten and positive aspects of out most ancient God. The Horned God provides the balance needed in this New Age, and he must be invoked as clearly and as ardently as the Goddess to whom he is twin.

This book shows how to make direct contact with your most ancient potentials, as exemplified by the Goddess and the Horned God. Using the simplest techniques *Earth God Rising* shows how we can create our own mystery and bring about real magical transformations.

0-87542-672-7, 256 pgs., 5-1/4 x 8, illustrated          **$9.95**

## GROWING THE TREE WITHIN
### by William Gray

The Qabalah is often considered the basic genetic pattern of Western esotericism. When we study the Qabalah, open ourselves to it and work with it as an Inner Activity, we gain wisdom that will illuminate our individual paths to perfection. Qabalah means "getting wise" in the broadest possible sense.

Formerly titled *The Talking Tree*, this book presents an exhaustive and systematic analysis of the 22 Paths of the Tree of Life. It includes a detailed and comprehensive study of the symbolism of the Tarot cards in which author William Gray presents a viable yet unorthodox method of allocating the Major Arcana to the Paths. Of particular interest is his attempt at reaching a better understanding of the nature of the English alphabet and its correspondence to the Tree of Life.

0-87542-268-3, 468 pgs., 6 x 9, illustrated          **$14.95**

## GODWIN'S CABALISTIC ENCYCLOPEDIA
### by David Godwin

This is the most complete correlation of Hebrew and English ideas ever offered. The practicing Cabalist or student no longer needs access to a large number of books on mysticism, magic and the occult in order to trace down the basic meanings, Hebrew spellings, and enumerations of the hundreds of terms, words, and names that are included in this book.

Included are: all of the two-letter root words found in Biblical Hebrew, the many names of God, the planets, the astrological signs, numerous angels, the Shem ha-Mephorash, the Spirits of the *Goetia*, the correspondences of the 32 Paths, a comparison of the Tarot and the Cabala, a guide to Hebrew pronunciation, and a complete edition of Aleister Crowley's valuable book *Sepher Sephiroth*.

Here is a book that is a must for the shelf of all Magicians, Cabalists, Astrologers, Tarot students, Thelemites, and those with any interest at all in the spiritual aspects of our universe.

0-87542-292-6, 528 pgs., 6 x 9                    $15.00

## THE GOLDEN DAWN
### by Israel Regardie

The Original Account of the Teachings, Rites and Ceremonies of the Hermetic Order of the Golden Dawn as revealed by Israel Regardie, with further revision, expansion, and additional notes by Regardie, Cris Monnastre, and others.

Also included are initiation ceremonies, important rituals for consecration and invocation, methods of meditation and magical working based on the Enochian Tablets, studies in the Tarot, and the system of Qabalistic Correspondences that unite the world's religions and magical traditions into a comprehensive and practical whole.

This volume is designed as a study and practice curriculum suited to both group and private practice—one of the most complete encyclopedias of Western Magick.

0-87542-663-8, 840 pgs., 6 x 9, illustrated        $19.95

Prices subject to change without notice.

## A GARDEN OF POMEGRANATES
### by Israel Regardie

What is the Tree of Life? It's the ground plan of the Qabalistic system—a set of symbols used since ancient times to study the Universe. The Tree of Life is a geometrical arrangement of ten sephiroth, or spheres, each of which is associated with a different archetypal idea, and 22 paths which connect the spheres.

*A Garden of Pomegranates* combines Regardie's own studies with his notes on the works of Aleister Crowley, A.E. Waite, Eliphas Levi and D.H. Lawrence. No longer is the wisdom of the Qabalah to be held secret! The needs of today place the burden of growth upon each and every person—each has to undertake the Path as his or her own responsibility, but every help is given in the most ancient and yet most modern teaching here known to humankind.
0-87542-690-5, 160 pgs., 5-1/4 x 8                    $8.95

## THE MIDDLE PILLAR
### by Israel Regardie

Between the two outer pillars of the Qabalistic Tree of Life, the extremes of Mercy and Severity, stands "The Middle Pillar," signifying one who has achieved equilibrium in his or her own self.

Integration of the human personality is vital to the continuance of creative life. Without it, man lives as an outsider to his own true self. By combining Magic and Psychology in the Middle Pillar Ritual/Exercise (a magical meditation technique), we bring into balance the opposing elements of the psyche while yet holding within their essence and allowing full expression of man's entire being.

In this book, and with this practice, you will learn to: understand the psyche through its correspondences on the Tree of Life; expand self-awareness, thereby intensifying the inner growth process; activate creative and intuitive potentials; understand the individual thought patterns which control every facet of personal behavior; regain the sense of balance and peace of mind that everyone needs for physical and psychic health.
0-87542-658-1, 176 pgs., 5-1/4 x 8                    $8.95

Prices subject to change without notice.

## MODERN MAGICK
### by Don Kraig

*Modern Magick* is the most comprehensive step-by-step introduction to the art of ceremonial magic ever offered. The eleven lessons in this book will guide you from the easiest of rituals and the construction of your magickal tools through the highest forms of magick: designing your own rituals and doing pathworking. Along the way you will learn the secrets of the Kabbalah in a clear and easy-to-understand manner. You will also discover the true secrets of invocation (channeling) and evocation, and the missing information that will finally make the ancient *grimoires*, such as the *Keys of Solomon*, not only comprehensible, but usable. *Modern Magick* is the perfect guidebook for students and classes. It will also help to round out the knowledge of long-time practitioners of the magickal arts.

0-87542-324-8, 608 pgs., 6 x 9, illustrated          **$14.95**

## SIMPLIFIED MAGIC
### by Ted Andrews

The qualities for accelerating an individual's growth and spiritual evolution are innate, but even those who recognize such potentials need an effective means of releasing them. The ancient and mystical Qabala is that means.

A person does not need to become a dedicated Qabalist in order to acquire benefits from the Qabala. *Simplified Magic* offers a simple understanding of what the Qabala is and how it operates. It provides practical methods and techniques so that the energies and forces within the system and within ourselves can be experienced in a manner that enhances growth and releases our greater potential. *A reader knowing absolutely nothing about the Qabala could apply the methods in this book with noticeable success!*

The Qabala is a system for personal attainment and magic that anyone can learn and put to use. The secret is that the main glyph of the Qabala, the Tree of Life, is *within* you. By learning the Qabala you will be able to tap into the Tree's levels of consciousness, and bring peace, healing, power, love, light and magic into your life.

0-87542-015-X, 208 pgs., mass market, illustrated          **$3.95**

Prices subject to change without notice.

## ARCHETYPES ON THE TREE OF LIFE
### by Madonna Compton

The Kabbalistic Tree of Life is the ageless mystical map to the secrets of the Universe. By working with its 10 circular paths and 22 linear ones, you can find answers to life's most profound questions. By mapping archetypes on the Tree, you can trace mythological and religious themes as well as those symbols that stir the psyche on deep inner levels. It can help bring out your latent powers and develop your full potential.

*Archetypes on the Tree of Life* symbolically examines the meanings and uses of the 22 paths based upon their correspondences with the Tarot trumps and Hebrew letters. The first half of the book is a scholarly approach to deciphering the archetypal symbols behind the etiology of the Hebrew letters, names and numbers. The second half is designed to enhance creativity and intuition through meditations and exercises that bring the material alive in the reader's subconscious.

0-87542-104-0, 336 pgs., 6 x 9, illustrated     **$12.95**

## A KABBALAH FOR THE MODERN WORLD
### by Migene Gonzalez-Wippler

If you have ever been intimidated by the Kabbalah in the past, and never studied its beauty, this is the book for you. It clearly and plainly explains the complexities of the Kabbalah. This is an ideal book for newcomers to the study of Kabbalah or mysticism and spirituality in general.

In this book, Gonzalez-Wippler shows that the ancient Kabbalists predicted the New Physics. She goes on to discuss such topics as: Planck's Quantum Theory, God and Light, Archetypes, Synchronicity, the Collective Unconscious, the Lemaitre "Big Bang" Theory, Einstein's Theory of Relativity and much more.

*A Kabbalah for the Modern World* unites psychology, physics and Western mysticism in such a clearly written form that it makes complex Kabbalistic ideas easy to understand.

0-87542-294-2, 256 pgs., 5-1/4 x 8, illustrated     **$9.95**

Prices subject to change without notice.

## THE NEW GOLDEN DAWN RITUAL TAROT DECK
### by Sandra Tabatha Cicero

The original Tarot deck of the Hermetic Order of the Golden Dawn has been copied and interpreted many times. While each deck has its own special flair, *The New Golden Dawn Ritual Tarot Deck* may well be the most important new Tarot deck for the 1990s and beyond.

From its inception 100 years ago, the Golden Dawn continues to be the authority on the initiatory and meditative teachings of the Tarot. Now, for the first time ever, a deck incorporates not only the traditional Tarot images but also all of the temple symbolism needed for use in the Golden Dawn rituals. This is the first deck that is perfect both for divination and for ritual work.

Meditation on the Major Arcana cards can lead to a lightning flash of enlightenment and spiritual understanding in the Western magickal tradition. *The New Golden Dawn Ritual Tarot Deck* was encouraged by the late Israel Regardie, and it is for anyone who wants a reliable Tarot deck that follows the Western magickal tradition.

**0-87542-138-5, 79-card deck & booklet**                    **$24.95**

## THE TEMPLE OF ISIS EGYPTIAN TAROT DECK
### by Ishbel

There are many Tarot decks on the market today, but according to Ishbel, the original Egyptian Tarot predates them all. This deck features the actual cards used by the Egyptians in 6000 B.C. The 22 Major Arcana cards depict the actual Egyptian deities—you will magically see the forces that determine your destiny. The 56-card Minor Arcana is composed of both picture and number cards.

Is someone working magic against you? Can you gain the affections of the person of your dreams? Use these cards to discover the answers to these and any other questions.

You will also learn to incorporate the Tarot with numerology, how to explore the ten levels of the Egyptian Tree of Life, and how to recognize the Egyptian Tarot as the forerunner of all modern Tarot decks.

**0-87542-333-7, 78-card deck & booklet**                    **$12.95**